THE NOBLE BEREAN

...AND THEY SEARCHED THE SCRIPTURES DAILY,
WHETHER THOSE THINGS WERE SO...

by

Thomas M. Kissinger

Straightway Publishing Company

Baton Rouge, Louisiana

The Noble Berean Series Volume 1

The Noble Berean:
And They Searched The Scriptures Daily,
Whether Those Things Were So

Copyright © 2008 by Thomas M. Kissinger
Straightway Publishing Company

All rights reserved. Any passage, except quotes, may be reproduced in any form whatsoever without permission from the author. All Scripture quotations are from the King James Version of the Bible unless otherwise noted.

For further information, contact the author through Straightway Publishing Company

Published by:
Straightway Publishing Company
Post Office Box 45212 #261
Baton Rouge, LA. 70895
Email: tkissinger01@cox.net
(225) 766-0896

Book and cover design: Rich Baldwin

The Noble Berean:
And They Searched The Scriptures Daily,
Whether Those Things Were So

By Thomas M. Kissinger

1. Author 2. Title 3. Inspiration 4. Religion
Library of Congress Control Number: 2007904055
ISBN: 978-0-9785134-1-2 (Paperback)

Printed in the United States of America

To my wife Sarah, and our children Moriah, Makayla, and Micah. I love you all and cease not to pray for you that God would give you the spirit of wisdom and revelation in the knowledge of Him! You are the sunshine of my life!

To Louis Thompson. I am amazed by your love for the true and living God and His righteousness!

To Billy Thompson. Thank you for teaching me to be a Berean!

To Dr. Harold Lovelace. You are a true Berean at heart. Thank you for all that you have invested into my life!

To Pastor David Davis. You and your wife are two of the most Christ-like people that I have ever met. Thank you for laying down your lives for the cause of Christ. You both have been a tremendous blessing to many people!

To Mary Cage. You have taught me many things. You are a great woman of God. Thank you for your many hours of editing!

> # GRAND STATEMENT
>
> *...they received the word with all readiness of mind, and searched the Scriptures daily, whether those things were so.*
>
> Acts 17:11

To all those who are Bereans at heart. I appreciate you for your willingness to receive God's Word with all readiness of mind. Continue to search the Scriptures daily!

To all those who are yet to be Bereans. You are invited to take a journey to the heart of the one and true living God!

CONTENTS

PART 1 – THE FALL, THE SACRIFICE, AND THE ORDER

PART 2 – 100 THOUGHT-PROVOKING QUESTIONS

PART 3 – DECEPTION

PART 4 – GOD'S GOVERNMENT

PART 5 – THE BODILY RESURRECTION OF THE LORD JESUS CHRIST

PART 6 – PERSECUTION

PART 7 – THE WHOLE COUNSEL OF GOD

PART 8 – THE DECREE OF THE MOST HIGH

PART 9 – THE GOD WHO RAISES THE DEAD

PART 10 – JESUS PAID IT ALL

PART 11 – THE NEW AGE MOVEMENT

PART 12 – THE LETTER VS. THE SPIRIT

PART 13 – THE HEART OF MAN

PART 14 – SONSHIP

PART 15 – THE LOVE OF GOD

INTRODUCTION

"As I have come to know Thomas Kissinger, his unique anointing has both blessed and amazed me. This young man proclaims the authentic Good News of Christ, the Successful Savior of all, in a manner that is unusually passionate, gentle-hearted, and clear. He is "upfront", yet compassionate and totally without bitterness or guile. His writing will stir you, enlighten you, strengthen your faith in God's never-failing love, and make the Bible literally "come alive" for you in ways you never could have imagined or foreseen.

Not only have I enjoyed Thomas' writings, I have admired his gracious manner of moving in the Spirit's wisdom when he answers those who oppose this message of infinite grace. I'm delighted to see how God is empowering Thomas to be a true leader and trumpeter of this true Gospel of Universal Salvation in this generation. I pray that (and believe that) our Heavenly Father will confirm His calling to many other young leaders in the days ahead through Thomas' life and ministry, and he will mentor many to do even greater Kingdom exploits that he himself will accomplish by the Spirit."

Sincerely and joyfully,
Charles Slagle

PART 1 - THE FALL, THE SACRIFICE, & THE ORDER

Ephesians 3:11 (Young's Literal Translation) states…"according to **a purpose of the <u>ages</u>**, which He made in Christ Jesus our Lord…"

In order to understand God, our existence, and the destiny of the human race, it is imperative that we delve into the purpose of God. We must first be enlightened to the fact that God has a purpose, and then we must see that His purpose is **A PURPOSE OF THE <u>AGES</u>!**

With this in mind, we are now able to gaze into God's purpose of the ages, looking for answers to the questions that have plagued mankind since the beginning of time. As was stated earlier, we must seek to find the answers to perplexing questions. We must ask ourselves…Who is God?...Why are we here?...What is our destiny (calling)? The key to answering these questions is to be found in an understanding of what the Bible refers to as the fall of man, the Supreme Sacrifice of the Lord Jesus Christ (His death, burial, and resurrection), and the order that is spoken of in 1st Corinthians 15:22-23, which states…"For as in Adam <u>all</u> die, even so in Christ shall <u>all</u> be made alive. **BUT EVERY MAN IN HIS OWN ORDER…**"

God's purpose of the ages is actually very simple, but has been greatly complicated by the ideas of religious men and women. After one comes to an understanding of the fall, the Sacrifice, and the order, God's purpose of the ages becomes *so elementary* that a wee child is able to understand it. So…Let us dig into and uncover God's purpose of the ages.

THE FALL

Romans 8:19 (The New Testament In Modern Speech) states…"For the Creation fell into subjection to failure and unreality (**not of its own choice, but by the will of Him Who so subjected it**)." WOW! Oh well…So much for "free will". As we can clearly see, GOD WAS RESPONSIBLE FOR THE FALL OF MAN! I know that some of you who are reading this right now are shouting…NO!...That is not correct! Nevertheless, it is the truth. Genesis 1:26-27 (King James Version) states…"Let Us make man in Our image, after Our likeness…" So God created man in His own image, in the image of God created He him; male and female created He them. It is important for us to **stop** here for a moment and meditate on what was just said. Did you happen to notice that God created man in His **own** image, and that He created him (man) male and female? Most casual readers of the Bible never catch what was just said. Here is what must be taken into account: God created man (the human race) in the spirit realm first before He placed him (beginning with Adam) into the earth realm. Notice that Adam was later **formed** of the dust of the ground in Genesis 2:7. It was at this time that Adam **became** a living soul. Remember…God breathed into the nostrils of Adam the breath of life and he became a living soul. In essence, the Adam of Genesis 1:26 was **lowered** into the soulish realm and **became** the Adam of Genesis 2:7. THIS IS THE FALL!!! The act of Adam's disobedience in his partaking of the tree of the knowledge of good and evil (his carnal mind) was just a result of being lowered (his subjection to failure and unreality) into the soulish realm **by God**. Many will ask the question…How can you say these things about God? The answer is simple. This is what the Bible actually teaches about the fall of man. I am simply repeating what the Bible states. Others would ask…Why would God do this to the human race?

Well…Let us go back to Romans 8:19-22. It tells us that God did this **in hope**, knowing beforehand that all those who were subjected to this vanity would be delivered from their bondage by the ministry and manifestation of the sons of God. In essence, God had predetermined to subject all to disobedience that He might have mercy on all through the cross of the Lord Jesus Christ (Romans 11:32). The cross of the Lord Jesus Christ was not an afterthought of God, but it was the very foundation and focal point of His entire purpose of the ages. Revelation 13:8 as well as 1st Peter 1:20 tell us that Jesus was the Lamb slain **from the foundation of the world!** This tells us that everything was built on the slain Lamb (Jesus Christ). God wanted the world to see Him as their Savior. The only way to accomplish this was to put man into the condition of needing a Savior. So…God did just that, for we know that all have sinned (missed the mark of God's nature) and come short of the glory of God (Romans 3:23). This can also be seen by applying the story of Job to the human race. Job was minding his own business when God asked Satan…Have you considered My servant Job? The rest of the story shows us that it was God Who subjected Job to everything that he went through. It tells us in Job 42:11 that it was the Lord Who was the One Who brought evil upon Job. AMAZING! Have you ever thought about that? Why did the Lord do this to Job? Our answer is to be found in Job 42:5 and 42:12. These verses tell us that Job had only heard of the Lord, but was now (because of everything that he went through) able to see **(understand)** the Lord. As well, verse 12 tells us that Job's latter end was more blessed than his beginning. And so shall it be with the human race. We shall all be able to see (**understand**) the Lord and our latter end shall be more blessed than our beginning as a result of having been subjected to the vanity that **God has placed us in**. What an AMAZING GOD that we serve!

THE SACRIFICE

It is now necessary to build upon our understanding of the fall of man by taking the next step, which step will bring us to a proper understanding of the Supreme Sacrifice of the Lord Jesus Christ. We will dissect why He had to die, which also tells us why He died, and we will also bring out what it truly is that His death has saved us from. In order to point out the true meaning of the cross of Christ, we must first expose the false teaching of Evangelical Christianity, which states that Jesus died on the cross to save us from eternal torture in hell. **THIS IS NOT CORRECT!** (As well, the hell of Evangelical Christianity is not the hell of the Bible. There is a difference, but that is another topic for another writing.)

So…Why did Jesus have to die? It is actually very simple. Think of it like this…The first Adam was disobedient, he sinned, and he died. The last Adam (Jesus Christ) was obedient, He never sinned, and He died. However, not only did He die, but HE ROSE FROM THE DEAD! So… We can now see that Jesus had to die to reverse the curse of Adam upon the human race. And so He did! Now…This leads us into our next two points, which speak of why He died and what His death saves us from. In simple terms, Jesus died to save us. The question is though, what has He saved us from? Our answer is to be found in Romans 6:23, which states…"For the wages of sin is death; but the gift of God is eternal life through Jesus Christ our Lord." Our next question should be…What is sin and death? The word "sin" means to miss the mark of God's nature and character and the word "death" speaks of the carnal mind, for the apostle Paul said that to be carnally minded is death (Romans 8:6). After having stated these things, we are now able to see that **JESUS DIED TO SAVE US FROM A CONDITION, NOT A LOCATION!** It is also vital that we understand that salvation is a **process**, and that we are being saved spirit, soul, and body (1st Thessalonians 5:23). This is also referred to as justification, sanctification, and glorification. This same thing can also be seen in type and shadow in the Old Testament in the three feasts of Israel, which were: Passover, Pentecost, and Tabernacles. In addition to all of this (and this is probably the most important point), **JESUS DIED TO MANIFEST THE LOVE OF GOD (1ST JOHN 4:9)!**

Remember...Jesus told His disciples..."*Greater love has no man than this, that a man lay down his life for his friends.*" To further explain the atonement of the Lord Jesus Christ I would like to include an excerpt from the writings of A. P. Adams. It is a real treasure of truth that must be considered by all.

According to A. P. Adams:

1. The atonement was not to satisfy God's Justice, but to reveal His Love.

2. The justice of God is not against the sinner, demanding his condemnation, but for him, insuring his salvation.

3. God is not in contrast with, much less in opposition to Christ in the atonement, but in perfect harmony and accord.

4. The atonement is not the exclusive work of Christ in order to reconcile God unto the world, but it is the work of "God in Christ" to reconcile the world unto Himself.

5. Christ does not have to plead with God in order to make Him willing to pardon the sinner, but God, by His ministers, "beseeches" (II Cor. 5:20) the sinner to make them willing to be pardoned.

6. Hence the atonement is not to propitiate God, but man; not to make God favorably disposed toward man, but to make His already existing favor known to man.

7. Christ did not die as our substitute, but as our companion and associate; not instead of man, but with him and for him.

8. Christ did not die to save us from the penalty of sin, but from sin itself.

9. Christ did not die that we might not die, but to deliver us out of a death in which we were already involved.

10. The sinner is not redeemed because he repents, but he is called upon to repent because he has been redeemed.

11. The atonement is not the cause of God's love to man, giving rise to that love, but the effect, flowing out of that love.

12. The final outcome of the atoning scheme is not a partial success,

but a perfect, absolute, and universal triumph! -end quote- (**The Atonement**, A. P. Adams)

THE ORDER

The last aspect that we will consider concerning God's purpose of the ages is what we will refer to as "the order". Many of God's people are not able to grasp this last point, but it is one of the keys that unlocks the mysteries of the Kingdom of God. Without an understanding of the order in which the human race is being brought to God through the cross of Christ, we are doomed to believe that God has all but lost the vast majority of the human race to eternal torments. As was stated earlier, **THIS IS NOT CORRECT!** Remember…1st Corinthians 15:22-23 says…"For as in Adam all die, even so in Christ shall all be made alive. **BUT EVERY MAN IN HIS OWN ORDER.**" Many would ask… How is this possible? Here is the answer: The Bible has three different categories of Scripture. There are Scriptures that speak of the **remnant (first-fruits), the nations, and all people and all things (the world).** These Scriptures must not be taken out of context and *must* be rightly divided! When we look closely at the Scriptures, we will see Scriptures that speak of a few being saved, all nations being saved, and finally, all people and all things being reconciled to God through the blood of the cross of Christ (Colossians 1:20). Is this a contradiction? NO! It is simply God's purpose of the ages. He has foreordained to save a remnant (first-fruits company) in this age, the nations in the coming age, and every other person and thing in the final age (the age of the ages / the dispensation of the fullness of times). These truths can be understood by studying the feasts of Israel, which speak of the barley harvest (Passover / the remnant), the wheat harvest (Pentecost / the nations), and the grape harvest (Tabernacles / the unbelievers). **THE FEASTS PROVIDE A KEY THAT UNLOCKS THE DOOR TO AN UNDERSTANDING OF GOD'S PURPOSE OF THE AGES!**

If we fail to see the order of God's great harvest, then we will fail to see the salvation of all men. It is actually so simple that it becomes hidden to the proud, but God is merciful and ever ready to remove the blindness that is caused by listening to our carnal minds and by believing the lies of religion. Many think that God's purpose will come to a close at the end of this age. OH HOW WE HAVE MISSED AND NOT DISCERNED THE PURPOSE OF OUR GOD! The first-fruits (the elect) is not the end of the harvest, BUT JUST THE BEGINNING. The first-fruits company will be used by God in the ages to come to gather in the remainder of the harvest. Please remember…This is only made possible because of the death, burial, and resurrection of the Lord Jesus Christ. The only reason there shall be a manifestation of the sons of God is because there was a manifestation of the Son of God. OH HOW GLORIOUS IT WILL BE. I do not have the vocabulary at this present time to proclaim just how marvelous it will be. We do know that the apostle Paul said that the sufferings of this present time are not worthy to be compared with the glory that shall be revealed in this first-fruits company. He referred to it as the MANIFESTATION OF THE SONS OF GOD! The church can say it isn't so. They can laugh in light of what has been stated in this teaching, but it will not stop God from going after the full amount of His purchased possession. He has paid for the human race through the precious blood of His Son Jesus Christ, and mark these words…HE SHALL BE SATISFIED! HE SHALL GET EVERYTHING THAT HE HAS PAID FOR! HE IS SOVEREIGN, ALMIGHTY GOD! HE CANNOT FAIL! HE WILL NOT FAIL! HE IS **THE SAVIOR OF THE WORLD!!!**

PART 2 - 100 THOUGHT-PROVOKING QUESTIONS

God has been asking man questions since the beginning of time. He started in Genesis 3:9 and has continued until the present. Why does God ask us questions? Why should we ask ourselves questions? Why should we ask others questions? Why did Jesus answer the questions that He was asked by the religious leaders in His day by asking them a question in return? The answer is simply this: God wants to engage man into the thinking process about Him. More importantly, God wants us to think about His **plan, purpose, power, and pleasure**. All the answers to God's questions can be found as one **diligently searches for the knowledge** of the previous statement. Without an understanding or knowledge of God's **plan, purpose, power, and pleasure,** these questions will certainly be very frustrating to the reader. On the other hand, if we search for an understanding of **the purpose of the ages,** we will be pleasantly surprised to find answers to all of these questions. All of the Holy Scriptures are of the utmost importance in your search, but there are certain **key Scriptures** that unlock the mysteries of the Kingdom of God. Here is one **key Scripture** to consider that will cause you to see God as **ALL IN ALL!** Keep this Scripture in mind as you answer each question…

Romans 11:36…"For **of** Him, and **through** Him, and **to** Him, are **ALL THINGS**: to Whom be glory forever. Amen."

ENJOY YOUR SEARCH!

1. Jesus told us to love our enemies. Does He love His enemies? Will He continue to love His enemies? If He ceases to love His enemies, would that make Him a hypocrite?

2. Is God able to save all men?

3. Does God want to save all men?

4. Can you tell me the meaning of the words: "Sheol," "Hades," "Gehenna," "Tartaroo?"

5. Can you tell me the meaning of the words: "Olam," "Aion," "Aionios?"

6. Did Jesus ever say the word "hell?"

7. What did the English word "hell" originally mean?

8. Is God vindictive or corrective?

9. Would you torture one of your children or loved ones forever?

10. What is accomplished by torturing someone forever?

11. Is the will of God stronger than the will of man?

12. Does God know the end from the beginning?

13. Did God know that Adam would fall?

14. Did Adam bring the entire human race into sin?

15. Did God send His Son Jesus to be the Savior of the world?

16. Did Jesus save the world?

17. Is Jesus the potential Savior of the world or the actual Savior of the world?

18. If all will not eventually be saved, how is it that we can call Jesus the Savior of the world?

19. Would you like for it to be true that all will be saved?

20. Did Jesus pay for the sin of the human race?

21. Will Jesus get everything He paid for?

22. It has been estimated that there have been about 160 billion people who have lived and died from Adam until the present. It has also been estimated that only about 5 billion of these people have been believers in Jesus Christ. If God starts out with 160 billion people and loses 155 billion of them to eternal torture, how can we say that God is victorious?

23. Did God lose the vast majority of the human race?

24. Was the first Adam more powerful than the last Adam?

25. Did Adam's fall bring down more people than the cross of Jesus Christ could save?

26. Has Jesus been defeated by Adam, sin, death, hell, and Satan?

27. Is the Devil more powerful than Jesus?

28. Did God create everything?

29. Did God create good and evil?

30. Did God create things for us to have to wrestle against?

31. Did God create the Devil?

32. What do the words "Devil," "Satan," and "Serpent" mean?

33. Who, what, and where is the Devil?

34. Is God in charge of the Devil?

35. Is God in charge of everything?

36. Why did Jesus die?

37. Why did Jesus have to die?

38. What did Jesus come to save us from?

39. What is salvation?

40. If the wages of sin is death, then why does Christianity teach that it is eternal torture?

41. What does it mean to be saved spirit, soul, and body?

42. What is justification, sanctification, and glorification?

43. What is the Kingdom of God?

44. What does it mean to "see" the Kingdom of God?

45. What was Jesus really saying in Luke 17:20-21?

46. What is Sonship?

47. What is the manifestation of the sons of God?

48. Is salvation a process?

49. What is the difference between spirit and soul?

50. Have you studied the feasts of Passover, Pentecost, and Tabernacles in the Old Testament? What do they represent for us today?

51. What does it mean to have the spirit of the law written on your heart?

52. Why do we go through trials?

53. Why are we afflicted by God?

54. Why do we suffer for Christ?

55. Why are we tempted?

56. Why do we pray?

57. What is the purpose of prayer?

58. How should we pray?

59. Is prayer for us or God?

60. Does our prayer change God's mind?

61. What does the Bible say about fire?

62. Is there such a thing as spiritual fire?

63. Is God going to burn people in eternal fire?

64. Did you know that the terms "Holy Ghost and fire," "God is a consuming fire," and "lake of fire" all speak of the same type of fire? Did you know that the fire in each one of these statements all comes from the same Greek word?

65. What is a fiery trial?

66. God makes His ministers a flaming fire! What does that mean?

67. God is a consuming fire! What does that mean?

68. We are to be baptized in the Holy Ghost and fire! What does that mean?

69. The Bible speaks of the lake of fire! What does that mean?

70. God's word is spoken of as fire in our mouths! What does that mean?

71. Who is Constantine? What impact did he have on Christianity?

72. Who is Augustine? What impact did he have on Christianity?

73. What are the Dark Ages? What impact did they have on Christianity?

74. What happened in 553 A.D. to impact Christianity?

75. Did you know that for the first 500 years after the resurrection of the Lord Jesus that the majority of the Church leaders taught that all would eventually be saved as a result of the cross of Christ?

76. Did you know that in the early church there were six schools of theology and that four taught the salvation of all men through Jesus Christ?

77. Who is Origen? What did he teach about the final destiny of all men?

78. The King James Version tells us that Jonah was in the great fish for three days and three nights and forever. Is that a contradiction? Are there any more contradictions in the King James Version? Should we look at some translations other than the King James Version to see if they are more accurate?

79. 1st Corinthians 15:28 says that God will be all in all. What does that mean?

80. Ephesians 1:9-11 speaks of the dispensation of the fullness of times. What is that?

81. 1st Corinthians 15:22 says that in Adam all die and that in Christ shall all be made alive, every man in his own order. What does that mean?

82. Colossians 1:20 says that there will be a reconciliation of all things because of the blood of the cross of Christ. What does that mean?

83. Acts 3:21 speaks of the restitution of all things. What does that mean?

84. Once again, Romans 6:23 tells us that the wages of sin is death. Why does Christianity teach that the wages of sin is eternal torture?

85. Jesus said in John 12:32 that if He would be lifted up from the earth (die on the cross) that He would draw (drag) ALL MEN UNTO HIMSELF! Why do Christians have a hard time believing that?

86. Is there anything too hard for the Lord?

87. What was the promise that God made to Abraham in Genesis chapter twelve?

88. Does that promise really mean "all?"

89. Have you read Psalm 22:27-31? That is some really good news!

90. What happens when God's judgments are in the earth? Here is a clue... Read Isaiah 26:9.

91. Could it be possible that God's judgment is a good thing?

92. Where does God's judgment begin? Here is a clue... Read 1st Peter 4:17.

93. Will God's wrath (wroth) last forever? Here is a clue… NO! Read Isaiah 57:16.

94. Will God's enemies submit themselves to Him? How much of the earth will worship Him? Read Psalm 66:1-4 to find out.

95. Will all flesh come to God? Read Psalm 65:2 to find out.

96. Will all nations serve God? Read Psalm 72:8-19.

97. Who has sent strong delusion? Read 2nd Thessalonians 2:11 to find out.

98. Since Jesus said that the end of this age would be characterized by false Christs, false prophets, and very strong deception, do you think it is possible that the majority of Christians are deceived?

99. Who is told to come out of Babylon (confusion) in Revelation 18:4?

100. **Since it has been prophesied that the end of this age would include strong delusion, deception, and confusion, do you think that we should question, study, look into, and challenge everything that we have been taught?**

PART 3 - DECEPTION

Deceive: to mislead by a false appearance or statement; delude.

According to Martin Zender:

"God purposely sends deceptions into the world—even in the form of mistranslated Scripture—to separate truth lovers from the lovers of injustice.

I'm glad you are here. I will quote you three Scriptures to support this initially disturbing point.

Proverbs 25:2—"It is the glory of God **to conceal** a matter, and the glory of kings to **investigate** a matter."

1st Corinthians 11:19—"**For it must be that there are sects (groups that deviate from accepted religious tradition) also among you**, that those also who are qualified may be becoming apparent."

2nd Thessalonians 2:11-12—"And therefore **God will be sending them an operation of deception**, for them to believe the falsehood, that all may be judged who do not believe the truth, but delight in injustice." -end quote- (Martin Zender Goes To Hell, Martin Zender)

GOD IS IN CHARGE OF DECEPTION

Could it be? Is it true? Is God in charge of deception? Is God the One responsible for sending strong delusion (an operation of deception)? YES! I know that this is troubling to many people who hear it for the first time, but nevertheless, IT IS THE TRUTH! How could it be any other way? Remember…God is sovereign. God is omnipotent (all-powerful), omniscient (all-knowing), and omnipresent (all-present). Is there anything that is not under His control? Is there anything that He is not in charge of? Is there anything that He does not either cause or allow?

DECEPTION IS PART OF GOD'S PLAN

Since deception is part of God's plan, then we must come to the conclusion that it is a necessary part of God revealing Himself to mankind. So…It is vital that we seek to understand deception, and that we also seek to understand why it is necessary. Before we do that, here are a few more Scriptures to support this point:

1st Kings 22:22-23—"And the LORD said, Who shall persuade Ahab, that he may go up and fall at Ramothgilead? And one said on this manner, and another said on that manner. And there came forth a spirit, and stood before the LORD, and said, I will persuade him. And the LORD said unto him, Wherewith? And he said, I will go forth, and I will be a lying spirit in the mouth of all his prophets. And He said, you shall persuade him, and prevail also: go forth, and do so. Now therefore, behold, **the LORD has put a lying spirit in the mouth of all these your prophets**, and the LORD has spoken evil concerning you."

Revelation 20:2-3—"And he laid hold on the dragon, that old serpent, which is the Devil, and Satan, and bound him a thousand years, And cast him into the bottomless pit, and shut him up, and set a seal upon him, **that he should deceive the nations no more, till the thousand years should be fulfilled: and after that he must be loosed a little season.**"

Revelation 20:7-8—"And when the thousand years are expired, **Satan shall be loosed** out of his prison, And shall go out **to deceive the nations** which are in the four quarters of the earth, Gog, and Magog, to gather them together to battle: the number of whom is as the sand of the sea."

Well…There you have it! There is no doubt that God is the One responsible for concealing things, creating sects, sending deception (strong delusion), putting lying spirits in the mouths of prophets, and shutting up and loosing Satan for the purpose of deceiving the nations.

WHY?

Why would God do these things? In order to understand something of this nature we must also be willing to accept that God created all things (good and evil, light and darkness, and opposing forces). This can be seen from such passages as Isaiah 45:7 and Colossians 1:16-20, as well as many other passages. The Bible is full of this kind of talk, but most never read the Bible, or they read it with their minds already made up and just ignore these types of passages, explaining them away.

Think of it like this…How could we know what truth was if there was no such thing as deception? How could we know what light was if there was no such thing as darkness? In fact, God starts everything in deception and darkness and then brings it to truth and light. Remember…Genesis 1:1-2—"In the beginning God created the heaven and the earth. And the earth was without form, and void; and **darkness** was upon the face of the deep. And **the Spirit of God moved** upon the face of the waters. And God said, **Let there be light**: and there was **light**."

With this in mind, we must grow up in our understanding of God. God has the power to shut us up in deception, and God has the power to illuminate our minds (give us ears to hear) to come out of deception and darkness into His marvelous light. It should be no surprise to us that the majority of the world (including the church) is in deception. GOD HAS PLANNED IT THAT WAY! As a matter of fact, Jesus told us that…there shall arise false Christs, and false prophets, and shall show great signs and wonders; insomuch that, **if it were possible, they shall deceive the very elect**.

WHERE DO WE GO FROM HERE?

After coming to a revelation such as this, we are now able to go from glory to glory, growing in grace and in the KNOWLEDGE of the Lord. We are able to approach all types of people, being all things to all men, that we might win some. We are no longer hindered by the traditions of men, which state that God is fighting against evil trying to do the best He can, but will lose the vast majority of the human race. On the contrary, God is in charge of all things, including deception. Deception is but another instructive tool in God's tool box, which is for the purpose of teaching man the difference between error and truth, and how to recognize those who are still in error, knowing that they have been placed there by God, and that we who have been brought out of deception by God are to (with love and compassion) lead the others out.

PART 4 - GOD'S GOVERNMENT

According to Bill Britton:

"It is absolutely necessary to have government, even in the things of God. Therefore, someone must be given authority by the Spirit. But authority is dangerous, unless the person with it has a heart full of compassion for others." -end quote- (Ten Dangerous Possessions, Bill Britton)

AUTHORITY WITHOUT COMPASSION

According to what was just stated, AUTHORITY WITHOUT COMPASSION IS A DANGEROUS POSSESSION! With this in mind, let us consider the government of God, comparing it to all other forms of government. We shall seek to prove that God's government is the highest and most effective form for governing the people of this earth.

GOVERNMENT

(From Wikipedia, the free encyclopedia)

"A **government** is a body that has the people to make, and the rulers to enforce rules and laws within a civil, corporate, religious, academic, or other organization or group. In its broadest sense, "to govern" means to rule over or supervise, whether over a state, a set group of people, or a collection of people. The government consists of different levels: local government, regional governments and national governments, depending on proximity to those who are governed and their responsibilities. The governments can be classified in various ways: Historically, classification has been according to the number of people who hold the power (one, a few, or a majority). More recently, classification bases itself on the institutional organization (parliamentary or presidential systems) or the distribution and the degree of control exercised over the society." (Wikipedia, the free encyclopedia)

FORMS OF GOVERNMENT

The five main forms of government are: **Anarchy, Capitalist, Communist, Democracy, and Dictatorship**. Anarchy exists when there is no government. Anarchists are people who believe that government is a bad thing. They say it stops people organizing their own lives. In a Capitalist or free-market country, people can own their own businesses and property. People can also buy services for private use, such as healthcare. But most Capitalist governments also provide their own education, health and welfare services. In a Communist country, the government owns things like businesses and farms. It provides its people's healthcare, education and welfare. In a Democracy, the government is elected by the people. Everyone who is eligible to vote has a chance to have their say over who runs the country. A Dictatorship is a country ruled by a single leader. The leader has not been elected and may use force to keep control. In a military Dictatorship, the army is in control. (The above information on forms of government was taken from CBBC Newsround.)

A CLOSER LOOK

There are many at this present time who would argue that a Democracy is the best form of government. As was stated, it allows the people to have their say and to live in freedom and liberty to make their own choices. With this being said though, Democracy does have its problems, and it is not a flawless form of government. It is a representation of the choices that are made by the people; but it does not necessarily mean that the choices that are made are righteous, morally correct, or in line with the law of God. A Democracy is an indicator of what is in the minds and hearts of the people who belong to that Democracy, but it does not necessarily mean that the minds and hearts of those people are in line with God. Just because someone is free to make a choice, does not mean that the choice that is made is according to the law of God. In no way is a Democracy a bad thing, for it is ordained of God for this present age and time, BUT IT IS NOT THE BEST THING. The best form of government has always been, is, and always will be THE GOVERNMENT OF GOD!

WHAT DO THE SCRIPTURES SAY?

Isaiah 9:6-7

"For unto us a Child is born, unto us a Son is given: and **the government shall be upon His shoulder**: and His name shall be called Wonderful, Counselor, The mighty God, The everlasting Father, The Prince of Peace. Of the increase of His government and peace there shall be no end, upon the throne of David, and upon His kingdom, to order it, and to establish it with judgment and with justice from henceforth even for ever. The zeal of the LORD of hosts will perform this."

The word "government" in this passage means rule and dominion. So… The question is…Where is this government? Why do we not see it? Why has it not taken over the earth? Where is this rule and dominion of the Lord Jesus Christ? Did not Jesus say…Thy kingdom (royal dominion) come…Thy will be done in earth, as it is in heaven? Well…YES HE DID! The key is to be found in discovering the true meaning and location of the Kingdom of God. Remember…Jesus told us (in Luke 17:20-21) that the Kingdom of God is within (inside) us. The Kingdom of God at this present time is to be found at work in the lives of those who are serving the Lord. It starts on the inside of man, working righteousness, peace, and joy into his very being. In essence, the government of God is His divine nature that is being written on the hearts of His people. It brings them from a fallen nature to a divine nature, causing them to put on the character and nature of their Father. It is quietly at work in the lives of the people of the Lord. This is not a Democracy. It is a THEOCRACY! According to Webster, the word "Theocracy" means: "government of a state by immediate **divine guidance** or by **officials** who are regarded as **divinely guided**." Are you ready for the truth? Can you handle it? In actuality, God's government is a DICTATORSHIP. There is a difference though, between His Dictatorship and the failed, evil Dictatorships of the world.

GOD IS A RIGHTEOUS DICTATOR!

It was Abraham who asked the question…Shall not the Judge of all the earth do right? What a question!!! The answer is…A RESOUNDING YES! The Scriptures declare over and over again that God and all His ways are righteous. In simple terms, this means that He is **right** in His character, nature, law, and all His ways. He alone is righteous! Not only is He righteous, but He is also a Dictator.

Daniel 4:34-35

"And at the end of the days I Nebuchadnezzar lifted up my eyes unto heaven, and my understanding returned unto me, and I blessed the Most High, and I praised and honored Him that lives for ever, Whose dominion is an everlasting **dominion**, and His **kingdom** is from generation to generation: **And all the inhabitants of the earth are reputed as nothing: and <u>He does according to His will</u> in the army of heaven, and among the inhabitants of the earth: and <u>none can stay His hand, or say unto Him, What do You do</u>?**"

This is definitely not the definition of a Democracy. Once again, these words explain the fact that our God is a righteous Dictator. His government is ruled by a single leader (Himself). He has not been elected, does not take votes, and is not interested in the opinions of men. He does according to HIS WILL! As well, He uses force when necessary to maintain control of His will and purpose in the earth. He also has an army. This army takes orders directly from Him and marches to the beat of His drum and His command. It is the army of the Lord. It is made up of those who have submitted themselves to His SOVEREIGNTY (INDISPUTABLE POWER).

AUTHORITY WITH COMPASSION

The word "Dictator" normally carries with it a negative connotation. The reason that God's Dictatorship is so effective is because HE IS LOVE! This means that God always does what is best for His creation, having the greater good in mind. He does what He pleases, but all of His ways are corrective in nature. It is this element (God's corrective love for all) that makes God's righteous Dictatorship the most pure form of government. The Dictators of this word have not been effective because they have not operated in righteousness and in the love of God. Evil Dictators are usually only concerned with what they want and what will profit them. God is not like that. He is moved with compassion, slow to anger, and full of mercy. He is touched with the feeling of our infirmities. Hebrews 4:15 states…"For we have not an high priest which cannot be touched with the feeling of our infirmities; but was in all points tempted like as we are, yet without sin." And again, Hebrews 2:9-10 states…"But we see Jesus, Who was made a little lower than the angels for the suffering of death, crowned with glory and honor; that He by the grace of God should taste death for every man. For it became Him, for Whom are all things, and by Whom are all things, in bringing many sons unto glory, to make the Captain of their salvation perfect through sufferings." Remember…"Behold, we count them happy which endure. You have heard of the patience of Job, and have seen **the end of the Lord; that the Lord is very pitiful, and of tender mercy** (James 5:11)." This means that the end goal of the Lord is that **He is extremely compassionate!**

THE INCREASE OF HIS GOVERNMENT

God's government is currently at work in His people, changing them and making them into the image of the Son of God. He sits on the throne of the hearts of those that serve Him now, but will eventually rule the hearts of all men. He comes to rule and reign with indisputable power, crushing that spirit of anti-Christ that now operates in the children of disobedience. He operates now in and through a first-fruits company that forms the Christ with Jesus as the Head. This first-fruits company is the army of the Lord that is the vessel through which His government shall continue to increase, until it consumes all men and all things, FOR GOD SHALL BE ALL IN ALL!

PART 5 - THE BODILY RESURRECTION OF THE LORD JESUS CHRIST

(Quotes assembled and put together by Thomas Kissinger)

According to John Gavazzoni: (After having been asked about the "supposed" tomb of Jesus that was said to have been discovered in Jerusalem)

"Over the last 53+ years of my spiritual experience in the faith of Christ, I've seen so many pseudo-scientific attempts to discredit the apostolic testimony, that it's just one more (yawn) blip on the screen for me as I relish the reality of the all-conquering Christ.

The bodily resurrection of Christ is certainly fundamental to the apostolic testimony and it is what gives content and cohesiveness to the meaning of God's purpose in creation.

The narrative of the resurrection of Christ recorded in the Gospels intersects with my experience of Him at the deepest level of my intelligence and subjective, intuitive awareness. All that is truly human in my existential psyche exclaims "He is risen; death is defeated; He makes all things new." -end quote-

According to Dr. Stephen Jones:

"The Scriptures as a whole find their focus upon Jesus. The hope of all mankind from the beginning to the end rests upon Him and His work and ministry. Thus, it is self-evident that the concept of resurrection in both the Old Testament and the new should be defined and understood in terms of Jesus' resurrection. Whatever one says about resurrection, where one is raised from the dead to immortality, Jesus' resurrection is the only real pattern we have. All other patterns, while helpful, are limited, because those raised from the dead later died as mortals.

The Pattern of Jesus' Resurrection

The first and most important pattern is that Jesus was raised bodily from the tomb. The disciples came to the tomb to look for Him, but He had risen. His resurrection was NOT the same thing as His ascension, or going to heaven. It was a physical, literal event, "as He said" (Matt. 28:6). In other words, when Jesus talked of the resurrection prior to that time,

He meant to convey the literal meaning of the term, not a "spiritual" event in the sense that some take it.

The only real question is "with what body do they come?" (1 Cor. 15:35) Is the resurrected body physical or spiritual? The answer is: BOTH. He had a heavenly Father and an earthly mother, and the resurrected body was the culmination of that relationship. He could enter the spiritual dimension ("heaven") or the physical, earthly dimension at will. His Father had given Him all authority in BOTH realms, even as He said in Matt. 28:18 (NASB), 18 . . . All authority has been given to Me in heaven and on earth.

As a result, He could take a physical form where the disciples could touch Him and see the wounds of His crucifixion (John 20:27). He could also eat food with the disciples (John 21:13; Luke 24:43). Then He could vanish (Luke 24:31) just as suddenly by taking spirit form. The question of whether Jesus was merely a spirit or if He had physical characteristics is faced and answered squarely in Luke 24:36-43.

And while they [disciples] were telling these things, He Himself stood in their midst. But they were startled and frightened and thought that they were seeing a spirit. And He said to them, Why are you troubled, and why do doubts arise in your hearts? See My hands and My feet, that it is I Myself; touch Me, and see, for a spirit does not have flesh and bones, as you see that I have. And when He had said this, He showed them His hands and His feet. And while they still could not believe it for joy and were marveling, He said to them, Have you anything here to eat? And they gave Him a piece of a broiled fish; and He took it and ate it before them.

Jesus went out of His way to prove to them that He was not a spirit and that He had "flesh and bones." He showed the disciples His physical scars, which no spirit would have. Then He asked for something to eat. A spirit cannot eat physical food.

Most commentators point out the fact that Jesus said nothing about having blood. He only spoke of "flesh and bones." While this is certainly true, the greater truth that He was raised with a physical body is often overlooked. And yet this is Luke's prime focus in the passage above, because it was the main truth that Jesus was revealing to the disciples at that moment.

This is not to say that Jesus was limited by His flesh to the physical world. The marvel of the moment was that Jesus, though physical, could move just as freely in the spiritual dimension as well. He was not confined to the spirit world, nor was He limited to the physical world. He had free access to both, because, as we have already pointed out, He had all authority in both heaven and earth, the spiritual and the physical realms.

Jesus said to the Samaritan woman in John 4:24…God is Spirit; and they that worship Him must worship Him in spirit and in truth. The Father, in other words, has generally limited Himself to the realm of the spiritual world. Man is likewise generally limited to the physical world. But Jesus is the Mediator, the Bridge between heaven and earth. More than that, He is our resurrection Pattern, our Example, by which we can know our destiny as well. What He is, we are becoming, for He is our Forerunner.

Jesus is limited by neither the spiritual world nor the physical world. He has all authority in BOTH realms. And so, even though we do not know very much about the nature of the resurrected body, the Bible makes these essentials very clear, because the nature of His resurrected body has become the pattern for our own resurrected body." -end quote- (The Purpose Of Resurrection, Dr. Stephen Jones)

According to the apostle Paul: (1st Corinthians 15:1-10)

"Moreover, brethren, I declare unto you the gospel which I preached unto you, which also you have received, and wherein you stand; By which also you are saved, if you keep in memory what I preached unto you, unless you have believed in vain. For I delivered unto you first of all that which I also received, how that **Christ died for our sins according to the Scriptures; And that He was buried, and that He rose again the third day according to the Scriptures: And that He was seen of Cephas, then of the twelve: After that, He was seen of above five hundred brethren at once; of whom the greater part remain unto this present, but some are fallen asleep. After that, He was seen of James; then of all the apostles. And last of all He was seen of me also, as of one born out of due time.** For I am the least of the apostles, that am not meet to be called an apostle, because I persecuted the church of God. But by the grace of God I am what I am: and His grace which was bestowed upon me was not in vain; but I labored more abundantly than they all: yet not I, but the grace of God which was with me." -end quote-

According to Gary Amirault: (After having been asked about the "supposed" tomb of Jesus that was said to have been discovered in Jerusalem)

"What I have read is that we have here a couple of guys who are in for a quick, cheap buck at Easter season. There are usually a few Jews during this time who bring up something to discredit Christianity and since the media is controlled by Jews who would like to get Christianity off this planet, they will promote it big time even if it's a big hoax like the Davinci Code. The archaeologist who discovered it in the 1980's discredits them as frauds." -end quote-

According to Richard Wayne Garganta: (After having been asked about the "supposed" tomb of Jesus that was said to have been discovered in Jerusalem)

"A publicity stunt. A Jewish historian says they have found about 70 tombs marked like this. It was a very popular marking at that time." -end quote-

'Lost Tomb of Jesus' Claim Called a Stunt
Archaeologists Decry TV Film

By Alan Cooperman Washington Post Staff Writer
Wednesday, February 28, 2007; Page A03

Leading archaeologists in Israel and the United States yesterday denounced the purported discovery of the tomb of Jesus as a publicity stunt.

Scorn for the Discovery Channel's claim to have found the burial place of Jesus, Mary Magdalene and -- most explosively -- their possible son came not just from Christian scholars but also from Jewish and secular experts who said their judgments were unaffected by any desire to uphold Christian orthodoxy.

"I'm not a Christian. I'm not a believer. I don't have a dog in this fight," said William G. Dever, who has been excavating ancient sites in Israel for 50 years and is widely considered the dean of Biblical archaeology among U.S. scholars. "I just think it's a shame the way this story is being hyped and manipulated."

The Discovery Channel held a news conference in New York on Monday to unveil a TV documentary, "The Lost Tomb of Jesus," and a companion book about a tomb that was unearthed during construction of an apartment building in the Talpiyot neighborhood of Jerusalem in 1980.

James Cameron, the filmmaker who explored the wreck of the Titanic and directed an Oscar-winning feature film based on its sinking, is executive producer of the documentary. Its claims are based on six ossuaries, or stone boxes for holding human bones, found in the tomb.

The filmmakers contend that the inscriptions on the boxes say Yeshua bar Yosef (Jesus son of Joseph), Maria (Mary), Yose (Joseph), Matia (Matthew), Mariamene e Mara (Maria the Master) and Yehuda bar Yeshua (Judah son of Jesus). They maintain that "Mariamene e Mara" is Mary Magdalene and that Yehuda bar Yeshua may be her son by Jesus.

Simcha Jacobovici, the film's Israeli-born director, said in a telephone interview yesterday that he commissioned four statistical studies that concluded that the odds of those particular names appearing in a single family tomb from the 1st century are "somewhere between 600 and 2.4 million to one."

Jacobovici also said tests on the patina, or surface residue, of the "James Ossuary," which surfaced in 2002; indicate that it also came from the Talpiyot tomb. Israeli authorities have pronounced the James Ossuary, which purportedly held the bones of a brother of Jesus, a forgery and are prosecuting its owner. Jacobovici, who made a 2003 Discovery Channel film about it, maintains it is real.

Dever, a retired professor of archaeology at the University of Arizona, said that some of the inscriptions on the Talpiyot ossuaries are unclear, but that all of the names are common.

"I've know about these ossuaries for many years and so have many other archaeologists, and none of us thought it was much of a story, because these are rather common Jewish names from that period," he said. "It's a publicity stunt, and it will make these guys very rich, and it will upset millions of innocent people because they don't know enough to separate fact from fiction."

Similar assessments came yesterday from two Israeli scholars, Amos Kloner, who originally excavated the tomb, and Joe Zias, former curator of archaeology at the Israeli Antiquities Authority. Kloner told the Jerusalem Post that the documentary is "nonsense." Zias described it in an e-mail to The Washington Post as a "hyped up film which is intellectually and scientifically dishonest."

Jodi Magness, an archaeologist at the University of North Carolina at Chapel Hill, expressed irritation that the claims were made at a news conference rather than in a peer-reviewed scientific article. By going directly to the media, she said, the filmmakers "have set it up as if it's a legitimate academic debate, when the vast majority of scholars who specialize in archaeology of this period have flatly rejected this," she said.

Magness noted that at the time of Jesus, wealthy families buried their dead in tombs cut by hand from solid rock, putting the bones in niches in the walls and then, later, transferring them to ossuaries.

She said Jesus came from a poor family that, like most Jews of the time, probably buried their dead in ordinary graves. "If Jesus' family had been wealthy enough to afford a rock-cut tomb, it would have been in Nazareth, not Jerusalem," she said.

Magness also said the names on the Talpiyot ossuaries indicate that the tomb belonged to a family from Judea, the area around Jerusalem, where people were known by their first name and father's name. As Galileans, Jesus and his family members would have used their first name and home town, she said. "This whole case [for the tomb of Jesus] is flawed from beginning to end," she said. -end of article- (<u>Lost Tomb Of Jesus Claim Called A Stunt</u>, Alan Cooperman)

TEN REASONS TO BELIEVE CHRIST ROSE FROM THE DEAD
One of the Essentials of the Christian Faith
(The Christian Arsenal / www.christianarsenal.com)

"1. The Public Execution By Roman Soldiers Assured His Death:

During the Jewish Feast of Passover, Jesus was swept away by an angry crowd into a Roman hall of justice. As He stood before Pilate, the governor of Judea, religious leaders accused Jesus of claiming to be the king of the Jews. The crowd demanded His death. Jesus was beaten, whipped, and sentenced to a public execution. On Golgotha outside of Jerusalem, He was crucified between two criminals. Brokenhearted friends and mocking enemies shared in His deathwatch. As the Sabbath neared, Roman soldiers were sent to finish the execution. These were professional executioners. To hasten death, they would break the legs of the criminals. But when they came to Jesus they did not break His legs, because from experience they knew He was already dead. As a final precaution, however, they thrust a spear into His side. It would take more than mere resuscitation for Him to ever walk about let alone be a threat again.

2. A Roman Official Sealed The Tomb:

The next day, religious leaders again met with Pilate. They said Jesus had predicted He would rise in 3 days. To assure that the disciples could not conspire in a resurrection hoax, Pilate ordered the official seal of Rome to be attached to the tomb to put grave robbers on notice. To enforce the order, soldiers stood guard. Any disciple who wanted to tamper with the body would have had to get by them, which wouldn't have been easy. The Roman guards had good reason for staying alert. The penalty for falling asleep while on watch was a brutal death.

3. The Grave Was Found Empty, In Spite Of Guards:

On the morning after the Sabbath, some of Jesus' followers went to the grave to anoint His body. But when they arrived, they were surprised at what they found. The huge stone that had been rolled into place over the entrance to the tomb had been moved, and Jesus' body was gone. As word got out, two disciples rushed to the burial site. The tomb was empty except for Jesus' burial wrappings, which were lying neatly in place. In the meantime, some of the guards had gone into Jerusalem to tell the Jewish officials that they had fainted in the presence of a supernatural being that rolled the stone away. And when they woke up, the tomb was empty. The officials paid the guards a large sum of money to lie and say that the disciples stole the body while the soldiers slept. They assured the guards that if the report of the missing body got back to the governor they would intercede on their behalf.

4. People Claimed To Have Seen Him Alive:

About AD 55, the apostle Paul wrote that the resurrected Christ had been seen by Peter, the 12 apostles, more than 500 people (many of whom were still alive at the time of his writing), James, and himself (1 Corinthians 15:5-8). By making such a public statement, he gave critics a chance to check out his claims for themselves. In addition, the

New Testament begins its history of the followers of Christ by saying that Jesus "presented Himself alive after His suffering by many infallible proofs, being seen by [the apostles] during forty days and speaking of the things pertaining to the kingdom of God" (Acts 1:3). Not only was He seen alive, but there were others who had died that were also resurrected and seen in Jerusalem (Matthew 27: 50 Jesus, when He had cried again with a loud voice, yielded up the ghost. 51 And, behold, the veil of the temple was rent in twain from the top to the bottom; and the earth did quake, and the rocks rent; 52 And the graves were opened; and many bodies of the saints which slept arose, 53 And came out of the graves after His resurrection, and went into the holy city, and appeared unto many.)

5. His Apostles Were Drastically And Permanently Changed:

When Judas Iscariot betrayed Jesus, the other apostles ran for their lives. Even Simon Peter, who earlier had insisted that he was ready to die for his Master, lost courage and denied that he ever knew Jesus. But the apostles went through a dramatic change. Within a short time, they were standing face to face with the ones who had crucified their Lord. Their spirits were bold and courageous. They became unstoppable in their determination to sacrifice everything for the One they called Savior and Lord. Even after they were imprisoned, beaten, threatened, and forbidden to speak in the name of Jesus, the apostles said to the Jewish leaders, "We ought to obey God rather than men" (Acts 5:29). After they were beaten for disobeying the orders of the Jewish council, these once cowardly and sheepish apostles "did not cease teaching and preaching Jesus as the Christ" (Acts 5:42). This was no mere story to save face. There were many men whom the Jews followed. They stirred up the people but were put to death and their fame and followers disappeared.

6. Witnesses Were Willing To Become Martyrs For Their Claims:

History is full of martyrs. Thousands and thousands of men and women have died for their belief in Jesus. For this reason, it is not that significant to point out that the first disciples were willing to die for their faith. But it is significant that while many will die for what they believe to be the truth, few if any will die for what they know to be a lie. That psychological fact is important because the disciples of Christ did not die for deeply held beliefs about which they could have been honestly mistaken. They died for their claims to have seen Jesus alive and well after His resurrection. They died for their claim that Jesus Christ had not only died for their sins but that He had risen bodily from the dead to show that He was like no other spiritual leader Who had ever lived. This is one of the most compelling reasons. It is one thing to say you believe something, but to die for it puts a whole different perspective on it.

7. It Was Clearly Predicted In The Old Testament:

The disciples were confused about some things. They expected their Messiah to restore the kingdom to Israel. Their minds were so fixed on the coming of a messianic, political kingdom that they didn't anticipate the events essential to the salvation of their souls. They must have thought Christ was speaking in symbolic language when He kept saying over and over that it was necessary for Him to go to Jerusalem to die and be resurrected from the dead. Coming from One Who spoke in parables, they missed the obvious until after it was all over. In the process, they also overlooked the prophet Isaiah's prediction of a suffering servant Who would bear the sins of Israel, being led like a lamb to the slaughter, before God "prolonged His days". (Isaiah 53:10)

8. The Day Of Worship For The Jewish Believers Changed:

Basic to the Jewish way of life was observing the Sabbath day of rest and worship. A Jew who did not honor the Sabbath was guilty of breaking the Law of Moses. Jewish followers of Christ began worshiping with Gentile believers on a new day. Being faithful to the Law was at the heart of the Jewish religion. They were fiercely devoted to their traditions. They were willing to die for them! The first day of the week, the day on which they believed Christ had risen from the dead, replaced the Sabbath. For a Jew, it reflected a major change of life. The new day, along with the Christian conversion rite of baptism, declared that those who believed Christ had risen from the dead were ready for more than a renewal of Judaism. They believed that the death and resurrection of Christ had cleared the way for a new relationship with God. The new way was based not on the law, but on the sin-bearing, life-giving help of a resurrected Savior.

9. It Was A Message That Changed The World:

Look at the course of history. The Gospel of Jesus Christ has raised and toppled empires. The promises of God throughout history can be clearly seen. Nations that have called upon God have been helped in their darkest hours. Nations that have refused to heed the message of the Gospel have suffered from the disease of sin and moral corruption to the point of extinction. You do not have to go too far in history to find out that a nation that falls has fallen from within. The mighty Roman Empire is a classic example. Look at the example we have today of the far-reaching effect of this message. Our calendar, our holidays, and many other parts of many of the world's cultures find their roots to this one all-important event in history. It can truly be said that this was the only important event in history for history is His Story.

10. It Fits The Experience Of Those Who Trust Him:

The apostle Paul wrote, "If the Spirit of Him Who raised Jesus from the dead dwells in you, He Who raised Christ from the dead will also give life to your mortal bodies through His Spirit Who dwells in you" (Romans 8:11). This was the experience of Paul, whose heart was dramatically changed by the resurrected Christ. It is also the experience of people all over the world who have "died" to their old ways so that Christ can live His life through them. This spiritual power is not evident in those who try to add belief in Christ to their old life. It is seen only in those who are willing to "die" to their old life to make room for the rule of Christ. It is apparent only in those who respond to the overwhelming evidence for Christ's resurrection by acknowledging His Lordship in their heart." -end of quote- (Ten Reasons To Believe Christ Rose From The Dead, The Christian Arsenal)

<u>HE</u> <u>IS</u> <u>RISEN!</u>

PART 6 - PERSECUTION

Have you been persecuted (pursued in a hostile manner, harassed) for righteousness' sake? Do people revile (speak abusively to) you? Are there those that say all manner of evil against you falsely for the sake of the Lord Jesus Christ? Well…<u>GREAT!</u> <u>WONDERFUL!!</u> <u>FANTASTIC!!!</u> It is time to **REJOICE!** As a matter of fact, you might want to plan a persecution party. You might even want to send a thank you card to your persecutors. You have just tapped into the highest level of maturity in the Kingdom of God. You are in the same class as the prophets which were before you. Jesus said that you are blessed.

BLESSED ARE THEY WHICH ARE PERSECUTED

Matthew 5:10-12 states…"Blessed are they which are persecuted for righteousness' sake: for theirs is the kingdom of heaven. Blessed are you, when men shall revile you, and persecute you, and shall say all manner of evil against you falsely, for My sake. Rejoice, and be exceeding glad: for great is your reward in heaven: for so persecuted they the prophets which were before you."

The Sermon on the Mount contains the words of life from our Lord and Savior Jesus. This Sermon takes us on a journey from poor in spirit all the way to being persecuted for righteousness' sake. As was stated at the beginning of this article, this is the highest level of maturity in the Kingdom of God. Persecution is important and necessary for our growth in God. Those who are putting on the divine nature (God's love) are able to respond to their persecution in a most peculiar way. They are actually glad that they have been persecuted for the sake of their Lord and are thankful for it. It causes them to rejoice in knowing that they were considered worthy to suffer shame for the name of Jesus.

In the book of Acts we are told that the apostles suffered a beating and were spoken evil of for speaking in the name of Jesus. Here was their response…"And they departed from the presence of the council, **rejoicing that they were counted worthy to suffer shame for His name**. And daily in the temple, and in every house, **they ceased not to teach and preach Jesus Christ** (Acts 5:41-42)."

ON THE RIGHT PATH

Persecution is a sure sign that you are on the right path. According to Luke 6:22-26, we are to be concerned when all men are speaking well of us. It states…**"Blessed are you, when men shall hate you, and when they shall separate you from their company, and shall reproach you, and cast out your name as evil, for the Son of man's sake. Rejoice in that day, and leap for joy: for, behold, your reward is great in heaven: for in the like manner did their fathers unto the prophets.** But woe unto you that are rich! for you have received your consolation. Woe unto you that are full! for you shall hunger. Woe unto you that laugh now! for you shall mourn and weep. **<u>Woe unto you, when all men shall speak well of you!</u> for so did their fathers to the false prophets."**

Did you hear what was just said? These amazing words from the lips of Jesus give us much knowledge concerning the subject of persecution. Once again, we are told to **REJOICE AND LEAP FOR JOY** when we are hated, shunned, and reproached. As well, we are also told that those who are never persecuted for the sake of Christ are FALSE PROPHETS. WOW! I think it is safe to say that those are very strong and piercing words. When was the last time you were persecuted for the cause of Christ? If you are not able to recall any times of persecution at all, YOU MIGHT WANT TO EXAMINE YOURSELF TO SEE WHETHER OR NOT YOU ARE IN THE TRUE FAITH OF CHRIST!

PERSECUTION FROM RELIGIOUS PEOPLE…THE REAL STUFF

Many people think that persecution is when some unbeliever mocks them, or when those in the world who are ungodly come against the idea of God, the Bible, and the Lord Jesus Christ. That, my friend, is **not** persecution. That is simply an unbelieving world manifesting a spirit of disobedience toward God that is within them until they are converted to the knowledge of God. True persecution comes from RELIGIOUS PEOPLE who are driven by a religious spirit, claiming to be something in God, when they are really not. This can be seen in the dealings that Jesus had with the scribes, Pharisees, and Sadducees (the religious leaders of His day). Those who are led by a religious spirit are always ready for a good fight. They are out for blood. They pick their prey and wait for the right time to pounce. They usually strike when they are in public, for they love the praises of men. If there is a way to make their victim look bad in front of others, this is their favorite method of battle. Sometimes though, they strike behind the back of the person, saying all manner of evil against them falsely, trying to discredit the person as much as they can. This is also an effective method for them to spew out their venom of self-righteousness. Jesus referred to these types of people as serpents and vipers.

WISE AS A SERPENT / HARMLESS AS A DOVE

So…How do we deal with these religious serpents and vipers? The key to dealing with these types of people is to be found in these three things: Love, Forgiveness, and Wisdom. Let me call to your remembrance how Jesus dealt with His hour of persecution. He said, "Father, forgive them; for they know not what they do." As we can see, He manifested the love and forgiveness of God in that He laid down His life, even for His enemies and those that persecuted Him. Jesus also told us to LOVE OUR ENEMIES! These are some of the most dramatic words ever spoken in history. In addition to operating in the love and forgiveness of God, we are to always lean on the wisdom of God. This enables us to be led by the Spirit, causing us to not cast our pearls before swine. There is a time to speak and a time to be quiet. There is a time to rebuke and a time to soothe. There is a time to stand your ground and a time to run for your life. Make no mistake about it. Religious people would love nothing more than to kill you and/or your message. Ultimately, God is our protector and refuge, a very present help in the time of trouble.

A PERSONAL TESTIMONY

Over the past several years God has graciously given me such a tremendous understanding of His purpose for the creation. He has introduced me to the spirit of wisdom and revelation in the knowledge of Him, taking me from glory to glory, and helping me to see that He is the actual Savior of the world, every man in his own order. I now see Him as all in all! He loses nothing. Not only has He gained back what the first Adam brought down (the human race), but He has far surpassed even that. The creation's latter end shall be GREATER than its beginning. There shall be a reconciliation of all things through the blood of the cross of Christ. It has begun with a remnant (first-fruits) in this age and shall continue with the nations and the unbelievers in the ages to come. "**O the depth of the riches both of the wisdom and knowledge of God! How unsearchable are His judgments, and His ways past finding out! For who has known the mind of the Lord? or who has been His counselor? Or who has first given to Him, and it shall be recompensed unto him again? <u>For of Him, and through Him, and to Him, are *ALL THINGS*</u>: to Whom be glory for ever. Amen. (Romans 11:33-36)**"

With all this in mind, you would think that family and friends would be eager to come by, sit down, and hear what it is that I have to say that has so radically changed my outlook on God and the final destiny of the human race. Well…NOT QUITE… Not only do most of them not show any interest, but they do not even ask a single question about what it is that has revolutionized my way of thinking. It is almost as though they are too scared to ask me anything. Most of them (except for the younger ones who have not been taken over by religion yet and are still open-minded) persecute me on a daily basis, speaking things about me that are not true. The funny thing is that they talk about me to others, but never come to me directly or even ask me one single question about what I believe. The other thing that is comical is that most of my persecutors would have a hard time explaining what they believe and would be hard pressed to find even one Scripture in the Bible to back up anything that they say. These people assume things about what I teach and continue to tell people to beware of me and to stay away. This has been hard on me and my wife, but we have come to understand that this comes with the territory. Oh well…What should we do?

REJOICE!!!

I am so excited about God that I hardly have time to think about my persecutors much (except to pray for them that God would have mercy on their blindness). As a matter of fact, I have never been more excited about God in my life. I love my persecutors and also forgive them for the ignorant words that they say. THEY KNOW NOT WHAT THEY DO OR SAY! I would rather spend my time rejoicing over THE GREATNESS OF GOD and also rejoicing that I have been found worthy to suffer shame for the glorious name and Gospel of Jesus Christ! To my persecutors, I say…"Thank you, hallelujah, and keep up the good work. You are helping me to overcome your religious spirit and to grow in grace and in the knowledge of the Lord. I will be here for you to love, forgive, and teach you when you are ready to humble yourself enough to come and learn of the ways of the Lord with a teachable spirit."

Oh how great our God is! He works all things together for the good of those that love Him and are the called according to His purpose. Rejoice in the Lord always: and again I say, **REJOICE!**

PART 7 - THE WHOLE COUNSEL OF GOD

Have you ever wondered why there are so many denominations, different groups, and divisions in the body of Christ? Why is this so? "Is there not one body, and one Spirit, even as we are called into one hope of our calling; one Lord, one faith, one baptism, one God and Father of ALL, WHO IS ABOVE ALL, AND THROUGH ALL, **AND IN US ALL** (Ephesians 4:4-6)?" If this is the case, then why do we see so much confusion, fighting, and separation in the church of the Lord Jesus Christ?

WE MUST EMBRACE ALL THE COUNSEL OF GOD

The reason for all of the separation that we just mentioned is due to the fact that most Christians do not embrace the whole counsel of God. They pick certain verses, passages, or themes out of the Bible and camp out on one particular thought or teaching from the Word of God. This is the reason for the insane number of denominations that have been established over the centuries. As a matter of fact, there are entire denominations and religions that are built on one or two Scriptures alone. Is that ridiculous, or what? In essence, they take one piece of the pie and call it the whole pie. This is a result of neglecting to embrace the whole counsel of God. The apostle Paul said in Acts 20:27, as he was speaking to the Ephesian Elders, "that he had not shunned to declare unto them all the counsel of God." The Amplified Bible says it this way..."For I never shrank or kept back or fell short from declaring to you the whole purpose and plan and counsel of God."

BALANCE

Man, because of his fallen nature, tends to be a creature of extremes, rather than a creature of balance. We all have the tendency within us to gravitate to the extreme in what we do and say. This causes us to embrace certain elements of God while we neglect other necessary and important elements of His Word. For example, most ministers of the Gospel tend to speak on the same subject or theme over and over again, neglecting to educate their listeners on the rest of the counsel (purpose) of God. Once again, this causes us to be unbalanced in our relationship with the Lord. We should strive to offer a balanced understanding of the counsel of God. Some ministers only talk about the here-and-now and others only talk about the future. Some only talk about money and others never say a thing about it. Still yet, some ministers believe in only focusing on the Scriptures (truth) while others believe in only focusing on worship (Spirit). Finally, some ministers only focus on positive Scriptures, such as healing, blessing, and receiving things from God, while others only focus on what seems to be the negative aspect of the Scriptures, such as punishment, vengeance, and wrath. CAN YOU SEE THAT WE AS THE PEOPLE OF GOD TEND TO BE OUT OF BALANCE AND THAT WE FALL SHORT IN THE AREA OF PROCLAIMING **THE WHOLE COUNSEL OF GOD**?

WHAT SHOULD WE DO?

According to the apostle Paul, we are to declare the whole counsel of God. Do you remember that Paul also spoke of being all things to all men? This means that we should be ready and willing to minister to people wherever they are at in their walk with the Lord. If they have never called on the name of the Lord, then teach them to call on the name of the Lord. If they have never been baptized in the Holy Spirit, then teach them about that precious experience. If they do not understand how to walk in victory on a daily basis, then teach them about partaking of God's divine nature. If they are not aware of the gifts of the Spirit, then bring these wonderful gifts to their attention. If they do not have an understanding of the ages or the reconciliation of all things, then teach them about ages and dispensations. If they do not understand the maturing process of the believer (sonship), then teach them about the sanctification of the believer. If they have never given finances to the work of the Lord, then teach them the importance of being a cheerful and willing giver…and so on…

The leadership (generally speaking) in the body of Christ has done a poor job in the area of delivering the whole counsel of God. It is very difficult to find those who are willing to teach all areas of the Word of God. Men would rather grab on to one aspect or truth from the Scriptures and camp out right there, not going into the fullness of God. The main reason for this is due to the fact that people love the praises of men and also love to stay where they are at in their understanding of the Lord. It is easier to "get all your ducks in a row", start a denomination, set all your beliefs in stone, and camp out right there until you build a mega-ministry. Many are content with staying where they are at in their understanding of the things of God. It is just like a child who does not want to grow up or hear that there is more to learn than what they have already been taught.

PREVIOUS MOVES OF GOD

Believe it or not, one of the biggest stumbling blocks that keep people from receiving the whole counsel of God is the previous thing that God has done or revealed to the body of Christ. We usually refer to this as a "move of God". For example, there have been moves of God that caused many people to come to repentance. There have also been moves of God that have brought the baptism in the Holy Spirit back to the forefront. As well, there have been moves of God that have brought people to the understanding of sonship. Finally, there have been moves of God that have caused people to be awakened to the purpose and plan of God concerning the ages to come, in which there shall be a reconciliation of all things. Each one of these sovereign moves of God is a part of His progressive revelation that is marching forth in the earth. They are building blocks that fit together as pieces in a puzzle to make a beautiful picture. The problem, though, is that man takes a particular truth or move of God and makes a denomination out of it. God has never meant for us to camp out on any one aspect of His truth, but to embrace all of it and to continue to build on top of the solid Rock, Who is the Lord Jesus Christ. **It is sad to say that the previous move of God always becomes the enemy to the next move of God.** This is man's fault, not God's fault. Whenever God begins to do a new thing there are always those from the previous move of God who will not budge or listen to the call of the Spirit to come up higher. They are the ones who actually fight against the new move of God, claiming that it is not of God because they do not see or understand what is being said. Remember when Paul began to bring in the doctrine of grace? There were so many people that could not grasp that God was doing a new thing. They so desperately wanted to hold onto the Old Covenant. Well…This is the same thing that the Gentile Church has done over and over again. It is all a result of being blind to the whole counsel of God.

TAKE HEED

The apostle Paul's closing words to the Ephesian Elders were words of warning that they should take heed concerning themselves and the flock over which God had put them in charge. The words "take heed" speak of keeping watch, or keeping up one's guard. The reason for this is that Paul knew that grievous wolves would come in with doctrines of demons and damnable heresies and would draw away disciples after them. So…How is it that we can guard against these types of religious wolves? Well…THE WHOLE COUNSEL OF GOD, OF COURSE!

Someone rooted and grounded in the whole counsel of God will not be swept away by every wind of doctrine that comes his way. He is one that is like a father in the faith, giving birth to spiritual sons who are also rooted and grounded in the Holy Scriptures. To say that we embrace the whole counsel of God proclaims that we embrace all the teachings of the Scriptures in their totality. It is a complete recognition and submission to the entire purpose and plan of God. It is the understanding of the person and work of the Lord Jesus Christ, and that all must come through Him, placing their faith in His death, burial, and resurrection for the forgiveness of their sin.

PART 8 - THE DECREE OF THE MOST HIGH

(Daniel 4:24-37)

Daniel chapter four tells us of a dream that King Nebuchadnezzar had. We are told that Nebuchadnezzar had a dream that made him afraid and troubled. As a result of his dream, he called for all the wise men of Babylon to come before him that they might make known unto him the interpretation of the dream. After exhausting the advice of all his magicians, astrologers, the Chaldeans, and soothsayers, he still was not able to find one who could interpret his dream. We are then told that Daniel came before him and that the king once again told his dream, hoping that Daniel would be the one to interpret it. The king went as far as to say that he believed that Daniel was the one to interpret the dream, for Nebuchadnezzar said to Daniel, "...but you are able; for the spirit of the holy gods is in you." Well...King Nebuchadnezzar was right. Daniel was the one!

It is important for us to recognize that this dream is not just history about the King of Babylon, but that it pertains to every person who has ever lived or will live. Besides the fact that this dream was specifically given to Nebuchadnezzar, it is a parable that is full of symbolic meaning that explains God's dealings with the human race. In essence, we are all as King Nebuchadnezzar. WE HAVE ALL BEEN PLACED UNDER THE DECREE OF THE MOST HIGH!

NEBUCHADNEZZAR

Before getting into the meaning of the dream it is important to also take note of the meaning of the king's name. "Nebuchadnezzar" means: "Nebo protect the crown". It also speaks of protecting one's border or frontier. So...What was is that Nebuchadnezzar was protecting? HE WAS PROTECTING HIMSELF, OF COURSE! He, along with every other human being who has ever lived, sought to protect his kingdom, his will, and ultimately, himself. He was not aware, though, that all that he had was given to him by God. This is the problem that exists in the heart of every man until it is dealt with by God. It is called "the pride of life". The lesson that Nebuchadnezzar was about to learn is the same lesson that we all must learn. God was about to show him that **THE MOST HIGH RULES IN THE KINGDOM OF MEN, AND GIVES IT TO WHOMSOEVER HE WILL!**

DRIVEN FROM AMONG MEN

Daniel begins the interpretation by telling the king that the dream is the decree of the Most High God. He then tells Nebuchadnezzar that the decree has come on him specifically. The word **"decree"** means: "a judicial decision or order." It also speaks of the eternal purpose of God and events that are foreordained. Not only did this decree come upon King Nebuchadnezzar, but it has come upon all who have ever lived or will live. It is the decree that has come upon the human race, whereby God has subjected the creation to vanity, not willingly (Romans 8:20). God has purposely lowered us into the soulish realm where we are subject to futility, frustration, and failure. He did this in hope, because the creation itself shall be delivered from the bondage of corruption into the glorious liberty of the children of God (Romans 8:21).

Daniel then tells the king that he shall be driven from among men for seven years, and that his dwelling place is to be with the beasts of the field, eating grass as do the oxen. This represents the fact that man has been driven from the spirit realm into the soulish realm, and that he has been given the nature or mark of the beast. This is also referred to as the sin nature or Adamic nature. It is the propensity in man to always gravitate to the ways of the flesh rather than the ways of the Spirit. Ecclesiastes 3:18-21 sheds much light on this subject. It states…"I said in my heart concerning the estate of the sons of men, that God might manifest them, **and that they might see that they themselves are beasts.** For that which befalls the sons of men befalls beasts; even one thing befalls them: as the one dies, so dies the other; yes, they have all one breath; so that a man has no preeminence above a beast: for all is vanity. All go unto one place; all are of the dust, and all turn to dust again. Who knows the spirit of man that goes upward, and the spirit of the beast that goes downward to the earth?"

God has purposely given us this beast nature that we might learn to overcome through the blood of the cross of Christ. We are being brought from the beast nature to the divine nature. As well, we are being brought from the mark of the beast to the mark for the prize of the high calling of God in Christ Jesus. Oh what a journey we are on! The decree of the Most High God has been placed on the creation for seven dispensations. This is the meaning of the seven years in the dream. The seven dispensations are: Innocence, Conscience, Human Government, Promise, Law, Grace, and Kingdom. The eighth dispensation is referred to by the apostle Paul as the dispensation of the fullness of times. It is during this time that God will make all things new, but for now, man is under the decree of the Most High God.

AFTER YOU HAVE LEARNED

As the interpretation continues, Daniel explains the part of the king's dream that included the command to leave the stump of the roots of the tree. He tells the king that his kingdom shall be sure to him after that he has learned and knows that the God of heaven rules. This part of the dream gives us great insight into the ways of God. It informs us of why God has subjected the creation to vanity, given us the beast nature, and afflicted us. Psalm 119:71 tells us that…"IT IS GOOD FOR US THAT WE HAVE BEEN AFFLICTED; **THAT WE MIGHT LEARN GOD'S STATUTES.**" Well…There you have it! God has placed the creation into its current scenario for the purpose of LEARNING that the God of heaven rules. How could it be any other way? How could we as sons and daughters of God become like our Heavenly Father without having to go through these trials and tribulations? Remember…Even the Son of God had to learn obedience through the things that He suffered (Hebrews 2:9-10).

REPENTANCE

After having given the king the interpretation of the dream, we now find Daniel telling the king that he must break off his sins and show the reality of his repentance. In order to begin a relationship with the Lord there is only one way. After having been drawn by the Lord, WE MUST REPENT. The word "repentance" means change. This change takes place in a person's life after they have been awakened by the Spirit of God to repent and believe on the Lord Jesus Christ. When we say "believe on the Lord Jesus Christ", what is it that we are actually saying? The answer is to be found in Romans 10:9-10. It states…"If you shall confess with your mouth the Lord Jesus, and shall believe in your heart that God has raised Him from the dead, you shall be saved. For with the heart man believes unto righteousness; and with the mouth confession is made unto salvation." In essence, we believe that Jesus died and rose again to save us from sin and death. We then place our faith in the person and work of the Lord Jesus Christ. Once again, true repentance is a work of the Spirit. A person who has truly repented has been dealt with by God. When this takes place it will manifest itself in the life of the person in the form of a lifestyle change. True repentance is not just a onetime thing, but it becomes a way of life to the believer. This is what places us in right standing with God. After having repented, we are justified by faith in the Lord Jesus Christ. Repentance is a twofold turning. It means to turn from sin and to turn to God.

THE ROYAL PALACE OF BABYLON

The Scriptures tell us that at the end of twelve months King Nebuchadnezzar was walking in the royal palace of Babylon. The king said, "Is not this the great Babylon that I have built as the royal residence and seat of government by the might of my power and for the honor and glory of my majesty? (Daniel 4:29-30)"

Let us take note of the meaning of the word "Babylon" before we go any further. The word "Babylon" means confusion or babble. This is where all men walk before they come to repentance and knowledge of the Lord. We have all walked (at one time or another) in the royal palace of Babylon. This is the place (spiritually speaking) where men walk around in religious darkness and confusion, being led by the carnal mind, thinking that they are God to themselves. It is in the royal palace of Babylon that man thinks that he has done everything by his power and might. It is the place of haughtiness, self-righteousness, ego, and pride that stinks to the high heavens. Don't worry, though…God is more than capable of humbling those that He has created. It only takes one touch from the Most High to bring a prideful man to his knees.

A VOICE FROM HEAVEN

Daniel 4:31 tells us "that while the words were still in the king's mouth, there fell a voice from heaven, saying, O King Nebuchadnezzar, to you it is spoken: The kingdom has departed from you…" This is the greatest thing that ever happened to the king. As a matter of fact, it is the greatest thing that could ever happen to anyone. This represents the beginning of our salvation process. It is the time when God strips us of our dependence on our ability and ushers us into a new dimension of learning to trust in Him. He takes away our kingdom (the things we have done outside of Him) and replaces it with His Kingdom. He takes away our will and replaces it with His will. As well, He takes away our beast nature (sin nature) and replaces it with His very own divine nature! Remember the conversion of Saul of Tarsus? Did he not also hear a voice from heaven? This is the way that God deals with men to come to repentance. You may not hear an audible voice, but you will surely hear that inner voice of conviction telling you to repent and believe on the Lord Jesus Christ.

THE END OF THE DAYS

Daniel 4:32-33 is the account of King Nebuchadnezzar actually living out the reality of the dream. Everything happened just as Daniel said it would. He actually became as a beast and ate the grass of the field for seven years. The Scriptures say that his hair grew like eagles' feathers and his nails were like birds' claws. All of this happened to the king, but not without hope.

At the end of the seven years Nebuchadnezzar lifted up his eyes to heaven, and his understanding and the right use of his mind returned to him. It is also said that he blessed the Most High God and praised and honored Him. This event introduces to us an incredible thought concerning the human race. It actually states that we were all with God in the beginning before being lowered into the soulish realm. It also states that there will come a time when all men (every man in his own order) will **REMEMBER AND RETURN TO THE LORD!** Psalm 22:27 states…"**All the ends of the world shall REMEMBER AND TURN to the Lord**…" Now let me ask you something. How can we remember something unless it is something that we once knew? As well, how can we return to someone (the Lord) unless we were with Him before? Do not the Scriptures say that "OF HIM, AND THROUGH HIM, AND TO HIM, ARE ALL THINGS (Romans 11:36)?" Think about it!

GOD DOES ACCORDING TO HIS WILL

The last three verses of Daniel chapter four give us the conclusion and result of all that the king was brought through. Nebuchadnezzar, who was once full of pride, has now been humbled to recognize the sovereignty and power of his Creator. The king states out of his own mouth that all the inhabitants of the earth are as nothing. He has also come to realize that "**God does according to His will** in the host of heaven and among the inhabitants of the earth, AND NONE CAN STAY (STOP OR HALT) HIS HAND OR SAY TO HIM, WHAT ARE YOU DOING (Daniel 4:35)?" That, my friend, is SOVEREIGNTY! This tells us that God's form of government is not a democracy, but a theocracy. God, Who is a righteous dictator, does according to His will. And thank God that He does, for all of His ways are just and right. Remember…God is love. So…We could say that our God is a righteous dictator Who is always motivated by love to bring the creation to the place where they will learn of His ways, and that their latter end shall be greater than their beginning.

The beautiful thing about all this is that it always results in man coming to the place where he has been brought from pride to humility. This is the goal of our God. It is not to destroy man, but to destroy that which is within man that keeps him separated from the knowledge of God. This is the process through which every person must come. We are all as King Nebuchadnezzar until dealt with by God. But rest assured…Our latter end shall be GREATER than our beginning. All men shall eventually be re-established and the right use of their minds shall return to them. We shall all with one accord "praise and honor the King of heaven, Whose works are all faithful and right and Whose ways are just (Daniel 4:37)." Remember…Those who walk in pride He is able to abase and humble.

PART 9 - THE GOD WHO RAISES THE DEAD

2nd Corinthians 1:8-11 states…"For we would not, brethren, have you ignorant of our trouble which came to us in Asia, that we were pressed out of measure, above strength, insomuch that we despaired even of life: But we had the sentence of death in ourselves, that we should not trust in ourselves, but in **God which raises the dead**: Who **delivered** us from so great a death, and **does deliver**: in Whom we trust that **He will yet deliver us**; you also helping together by prayer for us, that for the gift bestowed upon us by the means of many persons thanks may be given by many on our behalf."

This passage tells us two very important things that are useful to our growth in the Lord. We are first told that man is under the sentence of death. This is followed up by the good news that we have a God Who specializes in the raising of the dead. Herein lies man's problem and God's solution. Let us call to remembrance that "the wages of sin is death; but the gift of God is eternal life through Jesus Christ our Lord (Romans 6:23)." As we can see, man's problem is sin which leads to death, and God's solution is Jesus Christ which leads to life. With this in mind, let us attempt to define all the elements of death, burial, and resurrection.

THE SENTENCE OF DEATH

What is this "death" that the Scriptures speak of? When we say that "the wages of sin is death", what is meant by this? Well…We need to look no further than the words of the apostle Paul, for he plainly defines death for us in the book of Romans. Romans 8:6 gives us the clear and precise definition of the word death. It states…"**For to be carnally minded is death; but to be spiritually minded is life and peace.**" This is where we must begin our journey to understand such concepts as death, burial, and resurrection. It all begins here.

THE CARNAL MIND

Do you remember what God said to Adam in the book of Genesis concerning death? Genesis 2:16-17 tells us that "God commanded the man, saying, of every tree of the garden you may freely eat: But of the tree of the knowledge of good and evil, you shall not eat of it: for in that day that you eat thereof **you shall surely die**." Now…We know the rest of the story. We know that Eve was deceived and that Adam was disobedient. They both partook of the tree of the knowledge of good and evil. We also know that Adam and Eve (according to the Scriptures) did not physically die immediately after they did this. However, they did physically die later on. So…What does all this mean?

After taking all this into account, we are now able to come to the conclusion that the death that God was speaking of was first and foremost a spiritual death, causing man to live out of his soulish realm, which ultimately resulted in physical death as well. It was the death of the carnal mind that affected man's spirit, soul, and body. This death has placed man under the sentence of mortality. It is from this state that Adam and Eve fell. They fell from immortality to mortality which also resulted in them losing their glorified bodies. Do you recall that Adam and Eve did not know that they were naked until they had partaken of the tree of the knowledge of good and evil? This tells us that Adam and Eve were not just affected spiritually by this death, but also physically as well. The death that they were placed into by their actions caused them to be affected in their spirit, soul, and body. This is the reason why man must be delivered (raised) spirit, soul, and body.

Remember…TO BE CARNALLY MINDED IS DEATH! The words "carnal mind" speak of the fleshly mind or the corrupt nature of man. They also speak of man's ability outside of the Spirit of God. A person who is operating out of the carnal mind is one who trusts in themselves as opposed to trusting in the Lord. In essence, IT IS DEATH! Let us now attempt to look at how this death affects man in its totality. It actually affects our spirit, soul, and body.

SPIRIT, SOUL, AND BODY

1st Thessalonians 5:23 states…"And the very God of peace sanctify you wholly; and I pray God your whole **spirit** and **soul** and **body** be preserved blameless unto the coming of our Lord Jesus Christ." It is extremely important that we approach this subject in light of the fact that man is spirit, soul, and body. This is the only way to understand the totality of our resurrection experience out of death. We are being raised from the dead and it is happening in three phases. It is the resurrection of our spirit, soul, and body. As was stated earlier, we have **been delivered** (raised), we are **being delivered** (raised), and we are **yet to be**

delivered (raised). This speaks of our justification, sanctification, and glorification. The mistake that many people make is that they do not embrace the whole view of their resurrection experience out of death. It is not enough to just focus on one aspect of resurrection. WE MUST rightly divide the Scriptures concerning this topic. It is imperative that we teach all three aspects of resurrection, which include the raising of our spirit, soul, and body. This can be seen in type and shadow in the three main feasts of the Jewish people of the Old Testament. Their three main feasts were: Passover, Pentecost, and Tabernacles. These three feasts represent (on the individual level) the raising (or salvation) of our spirit, soul, and body. Take some time to study these feasts. You will see it for yourself. IT IS UNDENIABLE!

THE RELATIONSHIP BETWEEN SPIRIT, SOUL, AND BODY

According to Dr. Stephen Jones:

"When Paul speaks of "you entirely," he lists the three parts of "you." They are spirit, soul, and body. There is a difference between soul and spirit, which men can see if they rightly divide the Word of truth. Hebrews 4:12 says that "the Word is sharper than any sword and can divide soul and spirit." That alone shows that soul and spirit are two different things. They can be separated.

The best way to understand the relationship between spirit, soul, and body is to think of them in terms of their physical counterparts.

Spirit = breath, or wind [Heb. *ruach* = spirit, breath]

Soul = blood (Lev. 17:11)

Body = flesh (self-evident)

The breath gives oxygen to the blood, which is then carried by arteries and capillaries in the body. Even so, the spirit gives life to the soul, which is in the flesh. The relationship between spirit and soul is pictured in the relationship between the breath and the blood. They are different, but it is the spirit that gives life to the soul. It was only when God breathed the breath of life into Adam that he became a living soul.

When the breath is removed from a man, his flesh and blood dies. Even so, when God removes the breath of life from a man, *both his body and soul die*. A man's mind, will, and emotion cannot function apart from his flesh (brain). The out-of-body experiences that men often relate to us after being revived from death are not a function of the conscious soul, but of the consciousness of the spirit. As we will see shortly, the spirit and soul each have a separate consciousness.

The soul is not the part of man that transcends death. The soul comprises mind, will, and emotion that is dependent upon the Spirit of God for its existence and upon the physical body (brain) for its expression. It has a consciousness, as long as it is made alive by the breath or Spirit of God. When Spirit is separated from the body, it cannot survive, for James 2:26 says, "*the body without the spirit is dead*." But neither can the soul survive without the body, for it is mortal. The seat of life is in the spirit." -end quote- (The Judgments Of The Divine Law, Dr. Stephen Jones)

SPIRIT / …WHO "DELIVERED" US FROM SO GREAT A DEATH

The word "spirit" in the New Testament comes from the Greek word "pneuma" and refers to the wind or breath of God that is within us. As was stated earlier, it is the breath of life that is in us, making us a living soul. Due to the fall of Adam, man is born into spiritual death. It is the spirit of man that must first be raised out of this death in order for the soul and body to be raised as well. This is why Jesus told Nicodemus that a man must be born again in order to see (perceive) the Kingdom of God. When this takes place, man's spirit is raised out of death and into the life of God. We are raised with Him in newness of life and seated with Him in heavenly places. It is an awakening from the condition of sin, being brought into the first stage of the resurrection life of the Son of God. It is the raising of our spirit which brings us into an awareness of God and His Kingdom that was not previously there. The Bible refers to this as "justification by faith" (Romans 5:1). Oh what a glorious day it is when a person has that initial awakening out of death. This is brought about when the Spirit of God reveals to a person that he is a sinner and in need of a Savior. The Spirit of God then leads that person to repent and believe on the Lord Jesus Christ. It is wonderful, marvelous, and glorious! It is a new birth! The person's spirit has been raised. He has been delivered. As glorious as this is, God does not stop here. Not only has He delivered (raised) the person, but He *does deliver* the person. The deliverance (raising) continues, reaching forth to the soul.

SOUL / ...AND "DOES DELIVER"

The word "soul" in the New Testament comes from the Greek word "psuche" and refers to the mind, will, and emotions. The soul is the seat of our feelings, desires, and affections. It too must be raised or delivered from death. The soul, left to itself, will always lead man contrary to the ways of the Spirit. It must be dealt with by God. Once again, it must be raised! This is what it means when the Scriptures say that God *does deliver* us from death. Our deliverance is an ongoing process that continues past the initial salvation experience. It is referred to as "sanctification".

Romans 12:1-2 gives us insight into this process that is at work in the hearts and lives of believers. It states..."I beseech you therefore, brethren, by the mercies of God, that you present your bodies a living sacrifice, holy, acceptable unto God, which is your reasonable service. And be not conformed to this world: but be transformed by the renewing of your mind, that you may prove what is that <u>good</u>, and <u>acceptable</u>, and <u>perfect</u>, will of God." This passage of Scripture talks about the daily change that is taking place in the life of the believer. It is actually telling us of the transformation that takes place during the process of sanctification. As was stated, it is a renewing of the mind. The word "transformed" in this passage comes from the Greek word "metamorphoo". Does that word look familiar? How about...METAMORPHOSIS! Yes...We are undergoing a metamorphosis. In the same sense that a worm is transformed into a butterfly, we are being transformed (conformed) into the image of the Son of God. This is the salvation (raising) of our soul (mind, will, and emotions). During this process, God, by His Spirit, is writing His laws on our hearts so that we are to be no longer found as a worker of iniquity (lawlessness). Do you remember what was said in Jeremiah 31:31-33 concerning the law of God? In verse 33 it states..."But this shall be the covenant that I will make with the house of Israel; after those days, says the Lord, I WILL PUT MY LAW IN THEIR INWARD PARTS, AND WRITE IT IN THEIR HEARTS; AND WILL BE THEIR GOD, AND THEY SHALL BE MY PEOPLE." Well...This is what is taking place during our sanctification process. This is how God *does deliver* our soul from death. It is through continual submission to our fiery trials and tribulations that God accomplishes this. Keep this in mind...IT IS NOT ABOUT EFFORT, BUT SUBMISSION. God is the One doing the work, not us. We are but a yielded vessel. It is God Who is changing us, bringing us from glory to glory. Remember...We are God's workmanship (Ephesians 2:10)!

BODY / ...HE WILL "YET DELIVER US"

Not only does the spirit and soul need to be raised out of death, but the body must be changed as well. This is what Jesus, John, and the apostle Paul referred to as the "resurrection of the dead". The English word "resurrection" comes from the Greek word "anastasis". It is the same word that is used to describe the resurrection (anastasis) of the Lord Jesus Christ. There is also one instance in which the word "resurrection" comes from the Greek word "exanastasis". In both cases, these words are referring to the bodily aspect of resurrection. The Greek word "anastasis" is not referring to a spiritual awakening in the mind, but rather, it speaks of those who are in the invisible (Spirit) realm coming back into the visible (earthly) realm. The Bible actually speaks of two resurrections. We will discuss this later on in the article.

According to John Thomas, M.D.:

"Etymologically, *resurrection* is a *rising again*, from the Latin *resurgo*. In the Greek original of the New Testament it is represented by the noun anastasiV, as in Acts 24:15, where Paul, in his address to Felix, declares that he entertains the hope that there shall be a "resurrection of dead ones, both of just ones and also of unjust ones." This word *anastasis* signifies *a rising up, a standing up*; from *anisthmi, to stand up, or again, to cause to rise, etc.* The word *resurrection* occurs about forty times in the English Testament, but not once in the Old Testament, though the *subject* is amply set forth in "the Law and Prophets," only in other terms." -end quote- (<u>A Treatise On The Judgment Of The Dead At The Appearing Of Christ</u>, John Thomas, M. D.)

The final part of man that is to be raised is his body. It is the completion of his salvation process. This is what it means when the Scriptures state that God will *yet deliver us*. The resurrection of the dead (as it pertains to the body) has always been a highly debated topic down through history. This subject will always cause a division in a crowd of people. There are those who believe in the bodily resurrection of the dead and those who do not. It has always been this way. In the book of Acts chapter 23, verses 6-10, we are able to see just how controversial that this subject was in Paul's day. It states..."But when Paul perceived that the one part were Sadducees, and the other Pharisees, he cried out in the council, men and brethren, I am a Pharisee, the son of a Pharisee: **of the hope and resurrection of the dead I am called in question**. And when he had so said, **there arose a dissension between the Pharisees and the Sadducees: <u>and the multitude was divided</u>. For the Sadducees say that there is no resurrection**, neither angel, nor spirit: but the Pharisees confess both. And there arose a great cry: and the scribes that were of the Pharisees' part arose, and strove, saying, we find no evil in this man: but if a spirit or an angel has spoken to him, let us not fight against God. And when there arose a great dissension, the chief captain, fearing lest Paul should have been pulled in pieces of them, commanded the soldiers to go down, and to take him by force from among them, and to bring him into the castle." Well…I told you it was controversial. As a matter of fact, it is just about the same today. Bring this subject up in a diverse crowd of believers and see what happens. I wish it was not that way, but it is.

It is quite evident that the apostle Paul did believe in a bodily resurrection of the dead. (Read 1st Corinthians chapter 15.) He even goes as far as to say that if there is no resurrection of the dead, then Christ has not risen from the dead. In my opinion, it is just about impossible to read all of Paul's writings and not see that he taught a futuristic, bodily resurrection of the dead. There are some that object to the bodily aspect of resurrection BECAUSE THEY DO NOT UNDERSTAND THE NATURE OF THE BODY THAT IS TO COME FORTH. While there is much that we do not understand about the nature of the body of the resurrection, we do have the pattern of the resurrection of the Lord Jesus Christ Himself to look at. Jesus is the true pattern for all things pertaining to the human race, FOR HE IS THE PATTERN SON OF GOD!

THE NATURE OF THE RESURRECTED BODY

According to Dr. Stephen Jones:

"The first and most important pattern is that Jesus was raised bodily from the tomb. The disciples came to the tomb to look for Him, but He had risen. His resurrection was NOT the same thing as His ascension, or going to heaven. It was a physical, literal event, "as He said" (Matt. 28:6). In other words, when Jesus talked of the resurrection prior to that time, He meant to convey the literal meaning of the term, not a "spiritual" event in the sense that some take it.

The only real question is "with what body do they come?" (1 Cor. 15:35) Is the resurrected body physical or spiritual? The answer is: **BOTH**. He had a heavenly Father and an earthly mother, and the resurrected body was the culmination of that relationship. He could enter the spiritual dimension ("heaven") or the physical, earthly dimension at will. His Father had given Him all authority in BOTH realms, even as He said in Matt. 28:18 (NASB),

¹⁸ . . . All authority has been given to Me in heaven and on earth.

As a result, He could take a physical form where the disciples could touch Him and see the wounds of His crucifixion (John 20:27). He could also eat food with the disciples (John 21:13; Luke 24:43). Then He could vanish (Luke 24:31) just as suddenly by taking spirit form. The question of whether Jesus was merely a spirit or if He had physical characteristics is faced and answered squarely in Luke 24:36-43.

³⁶ And while they [disciples] **were telling these things, He Himself stood in their midst. ³⁷ But they were startled and frightened and thought that they were seeing a spirit. ³⁸ And He said to them, why are you troubled, and why do doubts arise in your hearts? ³⁹ See My hands and My feet, that it is I Myself; touch Me, and see, <u>for a spirit does not have flesh and bones, as you see that I have</u>. ⁴⁰ And when He had said this, He showed them His hands and His feet. ⁴¹ And while they still could not believe it for joy and were marveling, He said to them, have you anything here to eat? ⁴² And they gave Him a piece of a broiled fish; ⁴³ and He took it <u>and ate</u> it before them.**

Jesus went out of His way to prove to them that He was not a spirit and that He had "flesh and bones." He showed the disciples His physical scars, which no spirit would have. Then He asked for something to eat. A spirit cannot eat physical food.

Most commentators point out the fact that Jesus said nothing about having <u>blood</u>. He only spoke of "flesh and bones." While this is certainly true, the greater truth that He was raised with a <u>physical body</u> is often overlooked. And yet this is Luke's prime focus in the passage above, because it was the main truth that Jesus was revealing to the disciples at that moment.

This is not to say that Jesus was <u>limited</u> by His flesh to the physical world. The marvel of the moment was that Jesus, though physical, could move just as freely in the spiritual dimension as well. He was not confined to the spirit world, nor was He limited to the physical world. He had free access to both, because, as we have already pointed out, He had all authority in both heaven and earth, the spiritual and the physical realms." -end quote- (<u>The Purpose Of Resurrection</u>, Dr. Stephen Jones)

THE PURPOSE OF THE RESURRECTED BODY

Many would ask the question, why is there a need for a resurrected body? Well…Why was there a need for Jesus to be bodily resurrected? The answer has already been stated above and is actually quite simple. The purpose of the resurrected body is so that we will have (like Jesus) all power in heaven and in earth. This has always been the purpose of God from the beginning. God's purpose for man has been for him to have dominion over all things (except for God Himself, of course). The resurrected body is that which gives us authority and dominion over all things. This body will give us authority in the invisible realm as well as the visible realm. We will be able to be seen and able to vanish (go back to spirit). This is the same type of power and authority that Jesus had after His resurrection. It is with these bodies that the sons and daughters of God shall subdue all nations, bringing them to the knowledge of the Gospel of the Kingdom of God. These bodies will not be able to die or be destroyed. The sons and daughters of God shall be fully manifested in the earth, fulfilling the prayer of our Lord and Savior, when He stated… "THY KINGDOM COME. THY WILL BE DONE **IN EARTH**, AS IT IS IN HEAVEN." It shall truly come to pass that the meek shall inherit the earth.

THE FIRST RESURRECTION

Revelation 20:4-6 tells us of what the apostle John referred to as the "first resurrection". We are told that this resurrection will include those who were *"beheaded for the witness of Jesus, and for the Word of God, and which had not worshipped the beast, neither his image, neither had received his mark upon their foreheads, or in their hands…"* In simple terms, this speaks of those who have had their carnal minds replaced by the mind of Christ. These people have also had their nature changed from the beast nature to the divine nature. They have been brought from the mark of the beast to a life of pressing toward the mark for the prize of the high calling of God in Christ Jesus. This "prize of the high calling of God in Christ Jesus" is the first resurrection. Those that take part in this resurrection will rule and reign with Jesus Christ on the earth for 1,000 years. The apostle Paul referred to this as a "better resurrection" in Hebrews 11:35. He also referred to it in Philippians 3:11, saying…"If by any means I might attain unto the *resurrection of the dead.*" The word "resurrection" in this verse comes from the Greek word "exanastasis". It means: THE OUT-RESURRECTION FROM AMONG THE DEAD. This terminology refers to the first resurrection.

According to Dr. Stephen Jones:

"When God told Moses to build TWO trumpets in Numbers 10:2, He distinguished between the rulers and the congregation (Church). When Jesus, Paul, and John spoke of two resurrections in the New Testament, they added to the prophecy, showing that the rulers will be raised in the first resurrection, and the Church will be raised later in the second.

The apostle Paul continues this distinction in Philippians 3:10, 11, saying,

"That I may know Him [Christ], and the power of His resurrection and the fellowship of His sufferings, being conformed to His death; in order that I may attain to the resurrection from the dead [Greek: exanastasis ek nekron]."

Dr. Bullinger comments on this passage in his marginal notes in The Companion Bible. He tells us that the Greek word "exanastasis ek nekron" means OUT-RESURRECTION FROM AMONG THE DEAD. He says that the normal term used is simply "anastasis nekron," which is the resurrection of the dead--meaning all of the dead. But "EXanastasis EK nekron," he says, "implies the resurrection of some, the former of these two classes, the others behind left behind."

In other words, Paul was telling the Philippian Church that his desire was to attain the FIRST resurrection--the limited resurrection out from among the rest of the dead. Paul had no doubt that he would be resurrected. But he knew of a "better resurrection" (Heb. 11:35) that would occur 1,000 years before the general resurrection (Rev. 20:5). Paul did not doubt his salvation, but he did express concern that he might not attain this resurrection out from among the dead. Thus he continues in Phil. 3:12, saying,

"NOT THAT I HAVE ALREADY OBTAINED IT, or have already become perfect, but I press on in order that I may lay hold of that for which also I was laid hold of by Christ Jesus."

What is "it" that he had not yet obtained? He had certainly already qualified for the general resurrection as a citizen of the Kingdom. But he knew that "enduring to the end" was required to inherit the first resurrection and to rule with Christ during the thousand years of the Tabernacles Age.

So we see that understanding Moses' two trumpets opens up a whole new realm of prophetic understanding. It makes us more aware of the difference between a Passover Christian and a Tabernacles ruler ("the sons of God")." -end quote- (<u>Moses' Two Trumpets In Prophecy</u>, Dr. Stephen Jones)

THE SECOND RESURRECTION

Revelation 20:11-15 gives us the details concerning the second resurrection. John states…"And I saw the dead, small and great, stand before God; and the books were opened: and another book was opened, which is the book of life: and the dead were judged out of those things which were written in the books, according to their works…And whosoever was not found written in the book of life was cast into the lake of fire (verses 12 & 15)."

It is interesting to note that the book of life is present at the great white throne judgment. Why is this? Traditionally, the church has taught that only unbelievers will be present and raised in the second resurrection, but this is not correct. To the surprise of many, the second resurrection will include believers and unbelievers. If this were not the case, then why would it say…And whosoever was not found written in the book of life was cast into the lake of fire? It is obvious from this statement that there will be those in the second resurrection whose names are written in the book of life. Let us go to some other passages to clarify this further.

John 5:28-29 states…"Marvel not at this: for the hour is coming, in which all that are in the graves shall hear His voice, and shall come forth; they that have done good, unto the resurrection of life; and they that have done evil, unto the resurrection of damnation (judgment)."

Daniel 12:2 states…"And many of them that sleep in the dust of the earth shall awake, some to everlasting life (the life of the ages), and some to shame and everlasting contempt (the punishment of the ages)."

Acts 24:15 states…(The apostle Paul is stating his hope) "And have hope toward God, which they themselves also allow, that there shall be a resurrection of the dead, both of the just and unjust."

It is obvious that these passages are referring to the second resurrection, for we know that unbelievers are not going to be raised in the first resurrection. These Scripture passages state that there is a resurrection that will include both just and unjust people. So…These passages must be referring to the second resurrection.

1st Corinthians 3:11-15 gives us insight into how a believer will be dealt with who was not raised in the first resurrection. It tells us that "they shall be saved…yet so as by fire." The fire spoken of here is obviously symbolic of purification, for our God is a consuming fire. It tells us in verse 15 that…"If any man's work shall be burned, he shall suffer loss: but he himself shall be saved; yet so as by fire."

So…We can see that there is a difference in how the believers and unbelievers are dealt with in the second resurrection. The believers in the second resurrection are saved by fire and the unbelievers are cast into the lake of fire (a longer and more intense correction). The good news, though, is that God's fire is a spiritual fire (His fiery law) that is neither eternal nor vindictive in nature. It is for the purpose of correction and purification and is of the ages (age-lasting), not eternal.

CONCLUSION

The Scriptures testify that man is under the sentence of death, "for the wages of sin is death; but the gift of God is eternal life through Jesus Christ our Lord (Romans 6:23)." The Scriptures also attest to the fact that God is the One Who raises the dead. Finally, it is clearly stated in 1st Thessalonians 5:23 that man is made up of spirit, soul, and body, and that man must be sanctified totally and completely in his spirit, soul, and body. In essence, he must be raised from death in all of the three areas that were just mentioned. His spirit must be raised, as well as his soul and body. It could be said that **WE HAVE BEEN RAISED (JUSTIFIED), WE ARE BEING RAISED (SANCTIFIED), AND WE SHALL BE RAISED (GLORIFIED)!**

As was stated earlier in the article, there are many teachers of the Bible that only focus on one or two aspects of resurrection, but do not embrace the idea of man's need to be raised spirit, soul, and body. Understanding that we need to be raised in these three distinct ways is the only view broad enough to properly explain THE GOD WHO RAISES THE DEAD. Anything short of this is an attempt to isolate one area of God's purpose for man, not rightly dividing the Word of truth.

Oh what a loving, powerful, and wise God that we serve. He has placed all into death, subjecting the creation to vanity, not willingly. Even so, He shall raise all out of death. "For as in Adam **all die**, even so in Christ shall **all be made alive**. But every man in his own order (1st Corinthians 15:22-23)." HE IS THE GOD WHO RAISES THE DEAD!

PART 10 - JESUS PAID IT ALL!

There are many in the realm of Christianity who are familiar with the old Gospel song entitled "Jesus Paid It All". It was written by *Elvina M. Hall* in 1865 and put to melody by John T. Grape. It is one of the most adored Christian songs of all time. Here are the words:

I hear the Savior say,
"Thy strength indeed is small;
Child of weakness, watch and pray,
Find in Me thine all in all."

Refrain

**Jesus paid it all,
All to Him I owe;
Sin had left a crimson stain,
He washed it white as snow.**

For nothing good have I
Whereby Thy grace to claim,
I'll wash my garments white
In the blood of Calv'ry's Lamb.

Refrain

And now complete in Him
My robe His righteousness,
Close sheltered 'neath His side,
I am divinely blest.

Refrain

Lord, now indeed I find
Thy power and Thine alone,
Can change the leper's spots
And melt the heart of stone.

Refrain

> When from my dying bed
> My ransomed soul shall rise,
> "Jesus died my soul to save,"
> Shall rend the vaulted skies.
>
> Refrain
>
> And when before the throne
> I stand in Him complete,
> I'll lay my trophies down
> All down at Jesus' feet.

What a beautiful song that testifies of man's condition and God's solution. It trumpets the message of Christ and Him crucified as the answer for the lost condition of the human race. There is only one problem, though. Very, very few people actually believe what they are singing when they sing these words. In essence, the majority of those who sing this song would have to change the title of the song to… "Jesus *Potentially* Paid It All". The real question is this: If Jesus paid it all, **WILL HE GET EVERYTHING THAT HE PAID FOR?** Most who call themselves Christians would say that Jesus will not get everything that He paid for. The majority of those in Christianity believe and teach that about 95% of the human race will be lost, separated, punished, and tortured forever. So…They actually don't believe that Jesus paid it all. In actuality, they believe that Jesus potentially paid it all, but will not actually get everything that He paid for.

Have you ever paid for something and not gotten the full amount of what you paid for? How did that make you feel? Any sane person who paid for something with their hard earned money would go after the full amount of their purchased possession. If they were denied the full amount of what they had paid for, then they would probably bring the case to court in order to receive what was rightfully theirs. All of this is common sense to those of us who live in this world. For some reason, though, when it comes to God and what He has paid for through **the precious blood** of His Son Jesus Christ, most people are satisfied with believing that God is not interested in getting all of what He paid for. What causes us to come to such a ridiculous conclusion as this? What makes us think that God is not interested in the full amount of HIS PURCHASED POSSESSION, which is the human race in its entirety? How can we possibly say that Jesus paid it all and then turn right around and say that He will not get everything that He paid for? It is sad to say that most of the modern day church denies the fact that the Lord has bought us all.

DENYING THE LORD THAT "BOUGHT US"

2nd Peter 2:1-3 states…"But there were false prophets also among the people, even as there shall be false teachers among you, who privily (secretly) shall bring in damnable heresies, **even denying the Lord that bought them**, and bring upon themselves swift destruction. And many shall follow their pernicious ways; by reason of whom the way of truth shall be evil spoken of. And through covetousness shall they with feigned words make merchandise of you: whose judgment now of a long time lingers not, and their damnation (judgment) slumbers not."

These are some very strong words from the apostle Peter. I guess you could say that he knew how to peel the paint off of the wall (so to speak). Did you notice that Peter said that MANY would follow a false message by false teachers and that MANY would <u>deny the Lord that bought them</u>? This is definitely a description of the professing church of our day. The teachers in Christianity have (for the most part) denied that the Lord has bought us all. Most ministers teach that the Lord has bought us, but that we are able to cancel out what He has done by the power of our will. So…In actuality, those who teach such things do not believe in the sovereignty of God or that God has actually bought and paid for the human race. They believe that the will of man is stronger than the will of God and that God has only set Himself up to potentially acquire all that He has potentially paid for, but that God has not actually paid for all men, neither will He receive everything that He has paid for. In simple terms, they don't believe what they sing or teach about the Lord. They say that He has paid it all, but they really do not believe or understand what it is that they are saying. All of this deception is brought on by the false teaching of eternal torture.

THE BIG LIE

1st Corinthians 6:20 states…"For you are bought with a price: therefore glorify God in your body, and in your spirit, which are God's." What is it about statements like this that we do not understand? The sentence before this verse states that WE ARE NOT OUR OWN! We are plainly told that we do not belong to ourselves because that we have been bought and purchased by the Lord Jesus Christ. In light of this and what Peter said as well, how is it that we can read direct statements like these and still be convinced that God will not get everything that

He has paid for, and that He has all but lost the human race? The answer is: THE BIG LIE!

For approximately 1,500 years now the teaching of eternal torture has all but saturated the minds of those who call themselves Christians. It is the teaching that states that God sent His Son to be the Savior of the world, but He will not actually be able to save the whole world due to the fact that man's will is too strong for God to overcome. It is quite ironic that the people who teach this never stop to reason or think through what it is that they are teaching. When we teach that God cannot or will not save all men, we are teaching that He is weak and cruel, and that He has been defeated by sin, death, hell, and the grave. Is there any other possible conclusion?

The false teaching of eternal torture began to enter the hearts and minds of men in the days of Augustine (354 A.D. – 430 A.D.). He was actually very influential in bringing this pagan idea into the thoughts of Christian men and women. Prior to this time the majority of the early Church Fathers taught and believed in a reconciliation of all things through the blood of the cross of Christ. (Feel free to research this for yourself.) Is it any wonder that the world went into the Dark Ages shortly after Christianity began to embrace the idea that God's purpose was to save a few and to eternally torture the rest forever? **WHAT A DARK PICTURE OF GOD!!!** No wonder the world went into the Dark Ages.

Thank God that this teaching is a lie and that many are now coming back to an understanding of what the early Church Fathers believed and taught. This can be discovered by studying certain Hebrew and Greek words, such as: "Olam", "Aion", "Aionios", "Sheol", "Hades", "Gehenna", and "Tartaroo". One must also pray for the spirit of wisdom and revelation in the knowledge of God. Going to a Bible College will do more harm (in most cases) than good. After leaving these institutions, it causes a person to have to unlearn many things in order to grasp the true Gospel of the Lord Jesus Christ.

HE SHALL BE SATISFIED

Isaiah 53:11 states…"He shall see the travail of His soul, AND SHALL BE SATISFIED: by His knowledge shall My righteous Servant justify many; for He shall bear their iniquities." What could possibly satisfy our Heavenly Father more than having all His prodigal sons to come home? How could God be satisfied with the death of His only begotten Son unless He got everything that He paid for? We are told in verse ten that it pleased the Lord to bruise Him (Jesus). Why would God be pleased to see His only begotten Son crucified and put to death for the sin of the world? BECAUSE JESUS PAID IT ALL! As a result of His death, He shall draw (drag) all men unto Himself (John 12:32). Remember…"For as in Adam all die, even so in Christ shall all be made alive. **BUT EVERY MAN IN HIS OWN ORDER (1ˢᵗ Corinthians 15:22-23)…**" This is the key that unlocks to us the understanding of how Jesus will get everything that He paid for. The full amount of His purchased possession includes a remnant now (this age), the nations later (the coming age), and every knee and every tongue in the final age (the age of the ages).

CONCLUSION

If you are troubled by the things that have been said in this section of the book, I urge you to study and pray about what has been presented to you. Keep in mind that the Scriptures teach that Jesus paid it all. It would do you well to read Romans chapter five, paying close attention to what is being contrasted. Be sure to notice that what the first Adam brought upon all men has been REVERSED by the Lord Jesus Christ. What was it that Adam brought upon the human race? Well…Sin and death (mortality), of course. If this has been reversed by Jesus, which it has, then what would that mean for the human race? I think you can figure it out. Just remember…EVERY MAN IN HIS OWN ORDER!

<u>Jesus paid it all</u>,
All to Him I owe;
Sin had left a crimson stain,
He washed it white as snow.

PART 11 - THE NEW AGE MOVEMENT

It is sad to say that many in this day and age are leaving the Holy Scriptures to follow after the New Age Movement. This movement denies that the Holy Scriptures were inspired by God and that Jesus Christ is the only way to God. It will be our goal in this writing to expose the false teaching of the New Age Movement and to cause the reader to become aware of its negative consequences. Here is a detailed definition of the New Age Movement from *Christian Apologetics & Research Ministries* (www.carm.org):

"What is the New Age Movement?

a. The New Age Movement has many sub-divisions, but it is generally a collection of Eastern-influenced metaphysical thought systems, a conglomeration of theologies, hopes, and expectations held together with an eclectic teaching of salvation, of "correct thinking," and "correct knowledge." It is a theology of "feel-goodism," "universal tolerance," and "moral relativism."

b. In the NAM. Man is central. He is viewed as divine, as co-creator, as the hope for future peace and harmony. A representative quote might be: "I am affected only by my thoughts. It needs but this to let salvation come to all the world. For in this single thought is everyone released at last from fear." (A course in Miracles, The Foundation for Inner Peace, Huntington Station, N.Y. Lesson 228, p. 461.)

c. Unfortunately for the NAM. the fear they want to be released from might very well be the fear of judgment, of conviction of sin, and it is even, sometimes, fear of Christianity and Christians. Though the NAM. is tolerant of almost any theological position, it is opposed to the "narrow-mindedness" of Christianity that teaches Jesus is the only way and that there **are** moral absolutes.

d. The NAM. is difficult to define because "there is no hierarchy, dogma, doctrine, collection plate, or membership." It is a collection, an assortment of different theologies with the common threads of toleration and divergence weaving through its tapestry of "universal truth."

e. The term "New Age" refers to the "Aquarian Age" which, according to New Age followers, is dawning. It is supposed to bring in peace and enlightenment and reunite man with God. Man is presently considered separated from God not because of sin (Isaiah 59:2), but because of lack of understanding and knowledge concerning the true nature of God and reality." -end quote- (The New Age Movement, Christian Apologetics & Research Ministries)

THE HOLY SCRIPTURES

The first thing that those in the New Age Movement do is throw out their Bibles. If you happen to go to one of their meetings you will not see a Bible anywhere. This is done so that there will be no conviction of sin. New Age teachers aim to destroy the idea that there is anything such as absolute or spiritual truth. They embrace the idea that each person can literally have (come up with) their own truth, but that there is no such thing as there being one truth for all. In simple terms, this movement states that you can believe anything that you want to. In essence, you can do whatever floats your boat, cranks your tractor, or makes you feel all warm and fuzzy on the inside. Are you sick yet? I AM!

According to Keith Newman (Is God A Mathematician?):

"The authenticity of the Holy Bible has been attacked at regular intervals by atheists and theologians alike but none have explained away the mathematical seal beneath its surface.

It would seem the divine hand has moved to prevent counterfeiting in the pages of the Bible in a similar manner to the line that runs through paper money. Bible numerics appear to be God's watermark of authenticity.

Vital research on this numeric seal was completed by a native of the world's most renowned atheistic nation, Russia. Dr Ivan Panin was born in Russia on Dec 12, 1855. As a young man he was an active nihilist and participated in plots against the Czar and his government. He was a mathematical genius who died a Harvard scholar and a citizen of the United States in 1942.

Panin was exiled from Russia. After spending a number of years studying in Germany he went to the United States where he became an outstanding lecturer on literary criticism.

Panin was known as a firm agnostic - so well known that when he discarded his agnosticism and accepted the Christian faith, the newspapers carried headlines telling of his conversion.

It was in 1890 that Dr. Panin made the discovery of the mathematical structure underlining the vocabulary of the Greek New Testament. He was casually reading the first verse of the Gospel of John in the Greek: "In the beginning was the Word and the Word was with the God and the Word was God...".

Dr Panin was curious as to why the Greek word for "the" preceded the word "God" in one case and not the other. In examining the text he became aware of a number relationship. This was the first of the discoveries that led to his conversion and uncovered the extensive numeric code.

Dr. Panin found his proof in some of the oldest and most accurate manuscripts - the Received Hebrew Text and the Westcott and Hort Text.

In the original languages of the Bible, mostly Hebrew and Greek, there are no separate symbols for numbers, letters of the alphabet are also used to indicate numbers.

The numeric value of a word is the sum total of all its letters. It was curiosity that first caused Dr. Panin to begin toying with the numbers behind the texts. Sequences and patterns began to emerge. These created such a stirring in the heart of the Russian that he dedicated 50 years of his life to painstakingly comb the pages of the Bible.

This complex system of numbering visibly and invisibly saturates every book of the Scriptures emphasizing certain passages and illustrating deeper or further meaning in types and shadows. The 66 books of the Bible -- 39 in the Old and 27 in the New -- were written by 33 different people.

Those authors were scattered throughout various countries of the world and from widely different backgrounds. Many of them had little or no schooling. The whole Bible was written over a period of 1,500 years with a 400 year silence apart from the Apocrypha between the two testaments. Despite the handicaps the Biblical books are found to be a harmonious record, each in accord with the other.

Dr. Panin says **the laws of probability are exceeded into the billions** when we try and rationalize the authorship of the Bible as the work of man. He once said: "If human logic is worth anything at all we are simply driven to the conclusion that if my facts I have presented are true, man could never have done this."

"We must assume that a Power higher than man guided the writers in such a way, whether they knew it or not, they did it and the Great God inspired them to do it".

The Bible itself states clearly that it is the literal "God-breathed" living Word of the Creator. The words "Thus says the Lord" and "God said" occur more than 2,500 times throughout Scripture.

In 2nd Timothy 3:16 it states…"All Scripture is given by inspiration of God". Then in 2nd Peter 9:20-21 it plainly states…"No prophecy of the Scriptures is of any private interpretation. For the prophecy came not in old time by the will of man: but holy men of God spoke as they were moved by the Holy Ghost".

Let's take the number seven as an illustration of the way the patterns work. Seven is the most prolific of the mathematical series which binds Scripture together. The very first verse of the Bible…"In the beginning God created the heaven and the earth" (Gen 1:1), contains over 30 different combinations of seven.

This verse has seven Hebrew words having a total of 28 letters 4 x 7. The numeric value of the three nouns "God", "heaven" and "earth" totals 777. Any number in triplicate expresses complete, ultimate or total meaning.

Also tightly sealed up with sevens are the genealogy of Jesus, the account of the virgin birth and the resurrection. Seven occurs as a number 187 times in the Bible (41 x 7), the phrase "seven-fold" occurs seven times and "seventy" occurs 56 times (7 x 8).

In the Book of Revelation seven positively shines out: there are seven golden candlesticks, seven letters to seven churches, a book sealed with seven seals, seven angels standing before the Lord with seven trumpets, seven thunders and seven last plagues. In fact there are over 50 occurrences of the number seven in Revelation alone." -end quote- (Is God A Mathematician?, Keith Newman)

THE LORD JESUS CHRIST

The New Age Movement is a direct attack against the person and work of the Lord Jesus Christ. This is something that is to be found in all false doctrine. Every false teaching concerning God launches a direct attack against the person and work of the Lord Jesus Christ. If we do not embrace Christ and Him crucified, then we do not embrace the purpose and plan of God. As a matter of fact, the cross is the very foundation of all that God has done, is doing, or will do. The Scriptures tell us that "Jesus was the Lamb slain from the foundation of the world (Revelation 13:8)." The death, burial, and resurrection of the Lord Jesus Christ was not an afterthought to God, but it was the very foundation upon which He built His entire purpose of the ages. To read the Bible and not see that Jesus was God manifested in the flesh, and that Jesus proclaimed that He was the only way, would be the same as looking into the sky on a cloudless day and saying that you could not see the sun, or saying that the sun does not exist.

If we deny some of what Jesus said as being the truth but embrace other parts of what He said as truth, then we have denied all of what Jesus has taught. He is either the Messiah or He is not. There is no in between. If Jesus is not the way, the truth, and the life, then He is a liar, for He claimed to be the only way to the Father. We cannot embrace Him as just a good man alone. If He is the Messiah, then all of what He has taught must be embraced and conformed to. If He is not the Messiah, then we must discard all of what He has taught, for He would have to be declared as a liar. It doesn't work when we try to make Jesus one good man among others down through history, but strip Him of being the ONLY WAY to the Father. IT JUST DOESN'T WORK. IT DOES NOT HOLD WATER! John 10:7-9 states…"Then said Jesus unto them again, Verily, verily, I say unto you, I AM THE DOOR OF THE SHEEP. ALL THAT EVER CAME BEFORE ME ARE THIEVES AND ROBBERS: BUT THE SHEEP DID NOT HEAR THEM. I AM THE DOOR: BY ME IF ANY MAN ENTER IN, HE SHALL BE SAVED, AND SHALL GO IN AND OUT, AND FIND PASTURE."

In addition to all of this, when Jesus gave His disciples the Great Commission to go into all nations, He said…"Go therefore, and teach ALL NATIONS, baptizing them in the name of the Father, and of the Son, and of the Holy Ghost: TEACHING THEM TO OBSERVE ALL THINGS WHATSOEVER I HAVE COMMANDED YOU (Matthew 28:19-20)…" Jesus also told them to "go into all the world and preach the Gospel to EVERY CREATURE (Mark 16:15)." These statements declare that Jesus is the only way, for if He is not, then God would be contradicting Himself by sending the disciples into all the world to every creature with the Gospel of Jesus Christ while also accepting all other messages and "so-called gospels" as well. There cannot be more than one way to God in light of what the Scriptures teach. Why would God say that the only way is through His Son Jesus Christ and then also say that it does not matter who you come through or which path that you choose? It would defy reason and common sense for these things to be so. We cannot try to make God conform to us. We must SUBMIT and conform to His purpose and plan. The Scriptures also state that God is not the author of confusion. The idea that nothing matters and that you can pick your way to God IS CONFUSION! It is nothing but a lot of New Age "fluff". We must come to the realization that there is such a thing as SPIRITUAL TRUTH that must be conformed to.

SPIRITUAL TRUTH

In the same sense that there is such a thing as mathematical truth, THERE IS ALSO SUCH A THING AS SPIRITUAL TRUTH! Let's try to make this simple. We are going to cut through the chaos of the New Age Movement. For example…We know that $2 + 2 = 4$. This is a mathematical truth. There is no debate over this fact. We cannot change the outcome of $2 + 2$ no matter how hard we try. No matter where we live or who we are we cannot change it. $2 + 2$ will always $= 4$. We must conform to it. WE CANNOT MAKE IT CONFORM TO US OR MAKE IT OUT TO BE WHAT WE WANT IT TO BE. It is set! It is a mathematical truth! It is reality! Well…Now the spiritual.

Whether the New Age teachers want to recognize it or not, THERE IS SUCH A THING AS SPIRITUAL TRUTH! It cannot be invented or created. It can only be discovered or revealed. It is what it is whether we acknowledge it or not. Even if we are not aware of the truth it does not change it one bit. As well, if we deny the truth it does not change it one bit. As a matter of fact, the only thing that you can do with the truth is to believe it or not believe it. If this is the case, then we must seek to discover the truth about God, conforming to its every detail, not shunning it because we do not like some aspect of it. We must embrace the whole truth, asking God to reveal it to us through the Holy Scriptures. This is not to say that any one man has God's truth all figured out, but it is correct to say that there is such a thing as **absolute spiritual truth**, and that this truth is the same for every man. It cannot be otherwise! So… What is the truth? The truth is actually a Person. Well…You guessed it. Jesus is the way, THE TRUTH, and the life.

THE KNOWLEDGE OF CHRIST JESUS

Another pitfall to be found within the New Age Movement is that it does not recognize the excellency of the knowledge of Christ. The word "excellency" in Philippians 3:8 means to be superior or better than something else. The apostle Paul stated that he counted all things loss for the excellency of the knowledge of Christ Jesus his Lord, even referring to all other knowledge as *dung* in comparison to the excellency of the knowledge of Christ Jesus. This is not to say that other knowledge outside of the knowledge of God's purpose is bad or that it is wrong to acquire the knowledge of worldly things. It is simply stating that the knowledge of Christ is far more superior and better than any other type of knowledge. The New Age Movement places a great deal of emphasis on human intellect along with knowledge. The sad part, though, is that they do not recognize the excellency of the knowledge of Christ. It is quite ironic that some in this movement do not even believe in God. With all of their talk about education one would think that they would understand that IT IS IMPOSSIBLE TO HAVE CREATION WITHOUT A CREATOR. Oh well…Even though some of the New Agers do not believe in God <u>they cannot stop God from believing in them and Himself</u>. In due time He will have His way with all men.

THE CONSEQUENCES

It is important to point out that there are consequences for embracing the false teaching of the New Age Movement. Those who have divorced themselves from the Holy Scriptures and a belief in the One True God are headed down the wrong path. In simple terms (according to Jesus), they are trying to enter in another door other than the one God has provided (Jesus Christ) and climbing up some other way. Many in this movement (those who actually believe in God) are trying to achieve godliness outside of the Lord Jesus Christ. Jesus referred to this type of person as "a thief and a robber (John 10:1)." This type of thinking keeps one in his fallen condition, prolonging his subjection to vanity and the hell of the carnal mind. He thinks that he does not need to submit to the Lord and Savior Jesus Christ. He feels as though this is the freedom that he has been looking for his whole life. In actuality, this is not freedom at all. While it may feel good to his flesh for the time being, it is the same as a child who refuses to be disciplined and corrected by submitting to his parents. When the time comes for that child to be an adult he will not be ready for the task at hand. Since the child did not submit to the correction of his parents he is not able to face many of the things that life brings his way. His maturing process has been stifled by his rebellious spirit. It will take him many more years to become a man than if he would have just submitted himself to the loving correction of his parents who knew better than him.

This means that those who refuse to submit to the Lord Jesus Christ in this life are headed for further correction and purification in the ages to come. It is not that God is going to torture them forever, for that teaching is not correct. It does mean, however, that they shall suffer loss and lose their opportunity to rule and reign with Jesus Christ. Jesus put it this way in Luke 12:47-48…"And that servant, which knew his lord's will, and prepared not himself, neither did according to his will, shall be beaten with many stripes. But he that knew not, and did commit things worthy of stripes, shall be beaten with few stripes. For unto whomsoever much is given, of him shall be much required: and to whom men have committed much, of him they will ask the more." This is not talking about a literal beating, but it does refer to levels or degrees of correction. If you have been seduced by the New Age jargon please at least consider what has been stated in this brief teaching. It is impossible to come to God on any other terms than through the cross and shed blood of His only begotten Son Jesus Christ. Every other path is nothing but wood, hay, and stubble, which things are destined for the fires of purification in the ages to come. Let us conclude with the words of the apostle Paul…"For there is **one God**, and **one mediator** between God and men, **the man Christ Jesus**; Who gave Himself **a ransom for all**, to be testified in due time (1st Timothy 2:5-6)." AMEN!

PART 12 - THE LETTER VS. THE SPIRIT

The apostle Paul tells us in 2nd Corinthians 3:6 that "God has made us able ministers of the New Testament; **not of the letter, but of the spirit: for the letter kills, but the spirit gives life.**" It is <u>extremely important</u> that we seek to understand this statement that was made by Paul, for this is the key to being able to grasp the spiritual aspects of the Kingdom of God. So many people pick up the Bible and try to interpret it with raw intellect. They think that they can just read the Scriptures, using some type of formula to arrive at the meaning of what they are reading. For some, the Bible is viewed as systematic theology. For others, the Bible is only something to be looked at through the eyes of a Bible College professor. Still yet, others believe that only those with a degree from an institution are capable of properly interpreting the Bible. Well…Which one of these approaches is correct? The answer is…NONE OF THEM! So…Let's get to the solution.

THE VEIL

Further down in 2nd Corinthians chapter three, Paul, when speaking of the children of Israel, states that "their minds were blinded: for until this day remains the same veil untaken away in the reading of the Old Testament; which veil is done away in Christ. But even unto this day, when Moses is read, the veil is upon their heart." What is this veil that is spoken of in this passage? Well…It is none other than the carnal mind that Paul spoke about in Romans 8:6. Do you remember what it says? It states…"For to be carnally minded is death; but to be spiritually minded is life and peace." The words "carnal mind" speak of the corrupt nature of man. This refers to the fact that man is spiritually dead outside of being quickened (made alive) by the Spirit of God. It also refers to man trusting in his own way, knowledge, and ability. Paul calls it "being in the flesh". In order to begin our journey from the letter of God's law to the spirit of God's law we must first recognize the condition that we are in. It is a condition that produces a great gulf between us and God. It is the carnal mind versus the mind of Christ. You could also say that it is the flesh (man's ability) versus the Spirit.

THE OLD COVENANT VS. THE NEW COVENANT

The difference between the Old and New Covenants can be understood from reading Jeremiah 31:31-33. It states…"Behold, the days come, says the LORD, that **I will make a new covenant with the house of Israel, and with the house of Judah: Not according to the covenant that I** made with their fathers in the day that I took them by the hand to bring them out of the land of Egypt; which <u>My covenant they broke</u>, although I was a husband unto them, says the LORD: <u>But this shall be the covenant that I will make</u> with the house of Israel; After those days, says the LORD, <u>I will put My law in their inward parts, and write it in their hearts</u>; and will be their God, and they shall be My people."

After reading a passage like this it becomes clear to the reader that God has implemented two different covenants. The first one was based on man's performance. THE SECOND ONE IS BASED ON GOD'S PERFORMANCE. The first covenant, which was based on man's ability to keep the strict letter of the law, resulted in man breaking God's covenant. The second covenant, which is based on GOD (BY HIS SPIRIT) PUTTING THE SPIRIT OF THE LAW IN OUR INWARD PARTS AND IN OUR HEARTS, results in man actually becoming the people of God, for it states…"and I will be their God, and they shall be My people." This is what it means to go from the letter of the law to the spirit of the law. This transition takes place when GOD REVEALS TO US that we are incapable of knowing, serving, and loving Him apart from His Holy Spirit. It takes the revelation of the Spirit of God to bring us where we need to be in Him. The first covenant (man's ability to keep the strict letter of the law) was actually designed by God TO LEAD MAN TO THE BETTER COVENANT OF THE SPIRIT OF THE LAW. Listen to the words of the apostle Paul as he describes the difference between the two covenants. In Romans 8:1-5, it states…"There is therefore now no condemnation to them which are in Christ Jesus, who walk not after the flesh, but after the Spirit. For **the law of the Spirit of life in Christ Jesus** has made me free from **the law of sin and death**. For what the law could not do, in that it was weak through the flesh, God sending His own Son in the likeness of sinful flesh, and for sin, condemned sin in the flesh: **That the righteousness of <u>the law</u> <u>might</u> <u>be</u> <u>fulfilled in us</u>**, who walk not after the flesh, but after the Spirit. For they that are after the flesh do mind the things of the flesh; but they that are after the Spirit the things of the Spirit." Paul also told us that "the law (the letter) was our schoolmaster to bring us unto Christ (the Spirit), that we might be justified by faith (Galatians 3:24)." So…Where does this lead us?

THE SPIRIT

In order to experience God in all His fullness we must come to the realization that His life is only to be found in the Spirit. Outside of the Spirit of God there is only death. Remember…The letter KILLS, but the

Spirit gives LIFE! The mistake that people make is in thinking that they can come into a relationship with God by trusting in Him through the Spirit, but revert back to the letter of the law in the walking out of their Christianity. In essence, they come in by the Spirit, but they return to their own intellectual ability after that. That, my friend, WON'T WORK! THAT DOG JUST WON'T HUNT!

Do you remember how that the apostle Paul prayed for the believers at Ephesus? Do you remember what he prayed? Here is the prayer. It states…"That the God of our Lord Jesus Christ, the Father of glory, may give unto you the **spirit of wisdom and revelation in the knowledge of Him**: The **eyes** of your **understanding** being **enlightened**; that **you may know** what is the **hope** of **His calling**, and what the **riches** of the **glory** of **His inheritance** in the saints, And what is the **exceeding greatness of His power** to us-ward who believe, according to the working of **His mighty power**, Which He wrought in Christ, when He raised Him from the dead, and set Him at His own right hand in the heavenly places, Far above all principality, and power, and might, and dominion, and every name that is named, not only in this world, but also in that which is to come: And has put all things under His feet, and gave Him to be the Head over all things to the church, Which is His body, the fullness of Him that fills all in all (Ephesians 1:17-23)."

This passage of Scripture is telling us that WE MUST BE QUICKENED (MADE ALIVE) BY THE REVELATION OF THE SPIRIT OF GOD TO EVEN UNDERSTAND HIS PURPOSE AND PLAN. **WE MUST RECEIVE REVELATION FROM GOD! WE MUST HAVE THE SPIRIT OF WISDOM AND REVELATION IN THE KNOWLEDGE OF HIM!** This speaks of God unveiling Himself to us. In simple terms, you can be the most intellectual man on planet earth, but if you do not lean on the Spirit of God you will be absolutely clueless concerning spiritual things. You may think that your intellect is far superior to the knowledge of God, but you have declared yourself to be a fool by thinking that you can intellectualize your way into an understanding of spiritual things. So many Christians think that they can figure God out by going to some type of Bible College or by receiving a degree from a religious institution. WRONG, WRONG, WRONG! While you may learn a few things by spending time at a religious institution, you will have to spend more time unlearning many of the things that you have been taught to embrace the true purpose and plan of God. My advice to you is to get on your face and cry out to God for REVELATION TRUTH! Get yourself several Bible translations, a Concordance, and begin to pray for the spirit of wisdom and revelation in the knowledge of God, including the baptism in the Holy Spirit. THIS IS THE TRUE BIBLE COLLEGE THAT GOD WANTS YOU TO GO TO. I am not saying that it is wrong to go to man for help and explanation of the things of God, but if you do not seek God's revelation for yourself you are doomed to be saturated with the traditions and doctrines of men. The reason that most Christians are nothing more than modern day Pharisees is due to the fact that they are still trying to serve God by the letter of the law rather than by the law of the spirit of life in Christ Jesus. Since the letter kills, and they remain in the letter, their words kill rather than bring life. Most believers go around pointing a finger at others because they do not understand the difference between the letter and the Spirit.

THE FLESH PROFITS NOTHING

In John chapter six Jesus made some very startling statements. If they are not understood by the Spirit (the spirit of wisdom and revelation in the knowledge of Him), then they will cause the reader to become very alarmed. If these statements are received by the letter of the law, then they would probably cause the reader to turn back from following the Lord Jesus Christ. Jesus told His disciples that in order to follow Him that they would have to "**eat His flesh and drink His blood.**" He went on to say that if a person does not eat His flesh and drink His blood that they have no life in them. We are told later on in the chapter that His disciples, when they had heard this, said, "This is a hard saying; who can hear it?" Jesus, knowing their struggle with the statements that He had just made, gave them the key to understand what He had just said. He told them that "**it is the Spirit that quickens (makes alive); the flesh profits nothing: <u>the words that I speak unto you, they are spirit, and they are life</u>.**" According to the Spirit, Jesus was referring to us partaking of Who He was and what He would accomplish. This is what He meant when He said to eat His flesh and drink His blood. He meant for us to believe in Him and His death, burial, and resurrection. His statement spoke of Him giving His flesh for the sin of the world and that He would shed His innocent blood to take away our sin. He meant for us to partake (eat) of Him as the Son of Man, Son of God, and the Savior of the world. Well…There is our answer! THE LIFE OF GOD IS IN THE SPIRIT! Our fleshly efforts will always profit nothing as far as God is concerned. We may feel as though we have accomplished something great, but if it is according to the flesh it ultimately profits us nothing. As a matter of fact, God cannot be understood or embraced in His fullness according to the letter of the law. So many wonderful Christians who truly love God are **stuck** because they fail to recognize this all-important point. They continue to try to interpret the Scriptures by the letter of the law instead of praying for the spirit of wisdom and revelation in the knowledge of God. What would happen if we took these statements from Jesus in a literal sense? We would have to declare Him as slightly "off His rocker". After seeing that these statements must be understood by the Spirit, we can now see THAT THE ENTIRE BIBLE MUST BE UNDERSTOOD BY THE SPIRIT, FOR JESUS SAID THAT **HIS WORDS WERE SPIRIT AND THAT THEY WERE LIFE!** This is why it is so important that we do not lean on the natural man.

THE NATURAL MAN VS. HE THAT IS SPIRITUAL

The apostle Paul told us in 1st Corinthians 2:14-16 about the futility of the natural man (mind). It states…"But the natural man receives not the things of the Spirit of God: for they are foolishness unto him: neither can he know them, for they are spiritually discerned. But he that is spiritual judges all things, yet he himself is judged of no man. For who has known the mind of the Lord, that he may instruct Him? But we have the mind of Christ."

This passage of Scripture tells us that God does not reveal Himself to man through human intellect. It is by His Spirit that He unveils His Word to man. Paul also told us in 1st Corinthians 1:27 that "God has chosen the foolish things of the world to confound the wise; and God has chosen the weak things of the world to confound the things which are mighty." He even went on to say THAT NO FLESH SHOULD GLORY IN GOD'S PRESENCE. It is for this very reason that not many wise men after the flesh, not many mighty, not many noble, are called. Most who are extremely intelligent lean on their intellect instead of seeking God for REVELATION TRUTH. Once again, IT IS ONLY IN AND THROUGH THE REVELATION TRUTH OF THE SPIRIT OF GOD THAT WE CAN KNOW HIM AND UNDERSTAND HIS PURPOSE OF THE AGES!

RECEIVING REVELATION

One might ask the question…How do we receive revelation from God? Well…You could start by simply recognizing that you must have it and then ask God to give it to you. Yes…It is that simple. It is not hard to receive revelation from God, **but it does require humility and total dependence on the Spirit of God**. It could be said that desperation

<u>precedes revelation</u>. And so it is true. When we get desperate enough to want to know the true God we will cry out to Him for revelation truth. When we get sick and tired of being sick and tired of religion we will fall on our faces and ask God to reveal Himself to us. We will ask Him to show us not what we want to see, but we will ask Him to reveal His truth to us no matter what it takes. We will lose our own personal agenda and become swallowed up in His consuming fire. Then, and only then, will we be able to see past the letter of the law which kills, embracing the spirit of the law which brings life. Remember…"For the law of the Spirit of life in Christ Jesus has made us FREE from the law of sin and death. For what the law could not do, in that it was weak through the flesh, God sending His own Son in the likeness of sinful flesh, and for sin, condemned sin in the flesh: **THAT THE RIGHTEOUSNESS OF <u>THE LAW MIGHT BE FULFILLED IN US</u>, WHO WALK NOT AFTER THE FLESH, BUT AFTER THE SPIRIT** (Romans 8:2-4)!!!"

PART 13 - THE HEART OF MAN

The Bible is the story of the fall and rise of man. Within this story we are able to see that man has been subjected to vanity (futility) by God, not willingly (Romans 8:20). As a result of this, man finds himself in need of a Savior. And so we are told that "God so loved the world, that He gave His only begotten Son, that whosoever believes in Him should not perish, but have everlasting life (John 3:16)." In actuality, JESUS CAME TO THE EARTH TO DIE ON THE CROSS **TO SAVE US FROM A CONDITION**. To be blunt, this condition is brought on by our wicked hearts. The words "heart of man" speak of our inner man. The heart of man is the place or "seat" of his emotions, appetites, and passions. This is the part of man that is corrupt and in need of salvation. Jeremiah 17:9 states…"The heart of man is deceitful above all things, and *desperately wicked*: who can know it?"

Many would ask the question…How can we change the world and our condition? The answer is simple. To change the world, you must change the heart of man, ***STARTING WITH YOUR OWN!!!*** Can you imagine if every person in the world came to the realization that he was a sinner and in need of a Savior to change his heart? Can you imagine if every person began to focus on his fallen condition, bringing his wicked heart to the cleansing power of the Savior, working on his relationship with God, not pointing the finger or placing any blame on others for the way that he was? Well…This is the answer! Our problem is that we were born with a sin nature, which stems from having been subjected to vanity and a wicked heart. I know that upon hearing this for the first time that it leaves a person with many questions as to why the Lord would have placed us in this condition. There is a reason for God lowering us into this condition. The blessing is in **recognizing** the truth and reality of our current condition, and then in **discovering** and **submitting** to the solution (for our condition) that God has given us.

THE SIN NATURE

Whenever we try to diagnose the problem of the human race it is extremely important that we get to the **root** of our problem and that we also give the solution that goes to the very core of the problem. Many in the realm of Christianity mistake the symptoms of sin for sin itself. The symptoms of the sin nature are merely the **result** of the sin nature. So…It would have to be said that our sinful heart and the things that we do that come short of the glory of God are a direct result of the sin nature. This must mean that the root of our problem is the sin nature.

And so it could be said that sin, which means to miss the mark, is not so much what we do, but what we are. Sin is a fallen nature that we are born with that always causes us to gravitate to the ways of the flesh, which ways are always contrary to the ways of the Spirit of God. Man's problem is his inherent, fallen nature. In simple terms, our problem is sin, but sin must be understood in that it is a nature that causes us to come short of the glory of God, and its result is death (the carnal mind). Now…Let's get to the solution!

THE DIVINE NATURE

After having diagnosed the root of our problem it is easy to see what the cross of the Lord Jesus Christ was all about. Jesus, Who was God manifested in the flesh, came to die on the cross, manifesting the love of God, that we might be saved from our condition of sin which leads to death. He died to give us His life. As a result of Jesus dying on the cross, shedding His precious blood, being buried, and rising from the dead, we have (according to His divine power) "been given **ALL THINGS THAT PERTAIN UNTO LIFE AND GODLINESS**, through the **KNOWLEDGE** of Him that has called us unto glory and virtue: **WHEREBY ARE GIVEN UNTO US EXCEEDING GREAT AND PRECIOUS PROMISES: THAT BY THESE WE MIGHT BE PARTAKERS OF THE DIVINE NATURE, HAVING ESCAPED THE CORRUPTION THAT IS IN THE WORLD THROUGH LUST** (2nd Peter 1:3-4)."

If our wicked heart stems from the sin nature (our fallen nature), then surely the solution is the very divine nature of God Himself! Can you see the importance of understanding the meaning of this passage of Scripture? Can you see how many have not understood the simplicity of the Gospel? Can you see that there is but one problem and one solution for all men? It matters not what particular symptom of sin that one finds himself struggling with, there is really only one problem and one solution for all the shortcomings of those of the human race. The problem is our sin nature and the solution is God's divine nature. It is as simple as that!

Religion has complicated the simplicity of the Gospel of Jesus Christ. Religious men and women continually preach messages, trying to isolate all the different symptoms of sin, trying to give a separate solution for each one. It always results in them telling the people what they have to "do" in order to be free of that one particular symptom of sin, but always leaves the people burdened down, not being able to "do" what the preacher says, and actually makes them worse rather than better. This is the result of embracing the vicious cycle of playing church rather than partaking of God's divine nature. Can you see that there is a difference? Millions of Christians go to an altar at every church service, thinking that the mere act of going to an altar will somehow miraculously and instantly give them the victory that they need for the healing of their heart. While their intentions are good, they are beating their head against a brick wall, not realizing that it is the **knowledge of the truth** that will make them free. Remember…It is through the **knowledge** that we have been made partakers of the divine nature that we are able to escape the corruption that is in the world through lust.

PARTAKERS

Now that we have brought attention to the root of our problem (concerning the heart of man), let us now take hold of the glorious solution that God has given us for the healing of our sinful heart. As we have stated, our problem is our fallen nature, which leads to a wicked heart. Well…The solution is none other than God's divine nature, which leads to a pure heart. So…Kick off your shoes, sit down, and put on a pot of coffee. We are going to have coffee with the apostle Peter and see what he has to say about God's divine nature. Please take note of what he is about to tell you. He is going to give you the **key** that unlocks the door to a life of victory and overcoming power. He is going to tell you how to enter the everlasting Kingdom (the Kingdom of the ages) of our Lord and Savior Jesus Christ.

Imagine that you were to sit down with the apostle Peter to enjoy a cup of coffee and some fellowship in the things of the Lord. You would probably begin with some small-talk and then quickly move into a very serious conversation about the Lord. You would probably want to know what it was like to walk with Jesus and ask all about the miracles, signs, and wonders that were performed by the Lord and later by the apostles. My gut feeling is that Peter would spend some time answering those questions, but would quickly move to what he felt to be the very heart of God's Kingdom. Peter would want you to understand what it was that gave him and the other apostles the ability to live in victory and to turn the world upside down. He would begin (with great passion) to explain God's divine power that comes from His divine nature. He would explain man's condition, God's solution, and how to receive of that solution. You would surely hear Peter tell you of how that God brought him from a man who denied the Lord three times to a man that was able to heal people by his very shadow. After hearing his introduction you would definitely be ready for that second cup of coffee. You might even ask Peter to tell you about his ability to heal others by his shadow. You might say…Hey Pete…Tell me about this "shadow business". Peter would then reply…You better put on another pot of coffee…This is really going to get good!

Peter would start out by explaining to you that the word "shadow" in Acts 5:15 does not, in the original Greek, mean a dark spot made by the sun. The word means effulgence, radiance, a shining forth of divine energy. If it simply meant a dark spot caused by the sun, then on a cloudy day Peter would not have been able to be an instrument of God's healing power. In essence, Peter would explain to you that these "shadow healings" were a result of divine Holy Ghost energy. He would be sure to bring to your attention that it was not by his power, but by the divine power of Almighty God, stemming from God's divine nature.

Your next question for Peter would probably be…Hey Pete…What do I do to receive this divine power that comes from God's divine nature? He would certainly tell you…ABSOLUTELY NOTHING…IT IS NOT ABOUT DOING, BUT PARTAKING! He would tell you that you must learn to be a PARTAKER OF GOD'S DIVINE NATURE! To "partake" means to participate or operate in something that has already been provided for you. The great mistake of the modern day church is that it thinks that it can solve the heart problem of man and manifest the power of God by trying to do something for God. This is nothing but the flesh (man's efforts). We must learn that God has already given us ALL THINGS that pertain to life and godliness, including His power, through His divine nature. This is what Jesus purchased for the human race at Calvary. He bought us in order that we might be partakers of the divine nature. To "partake of God's divine nature" simply means to receive, participate, and operate in His prescribed solution for the heart of man. We are simply to receive and take on the nature of our Heavenly Father that has been provided for us through the person and work of the Lord Jesus Christ. God then works in and through us, burning up our wood, hay, and stubble, bringing us from the fallen nature to His very own divine nature. Peter would then tell you that this process (partaking of God's divine nature) is the very thing that gives you an entrance into the Kingdom of God and brings you to the place where you can <u>never</u> <u>fall</u>.

Just as you would go to a family celebration and partake of all the wonderful food that was there, you can also come to the Father's table (His nature) and partake of all the wonderful things that pertain to life and godliness. It is just that simple! We as Christians must stop making complicated what is actually very simple. God has made it possible for us to become sharers in His very nature. This alone is the only thing that will bring us from a wicked heart to a pure heart, causing us to manifest the life and power of God.

SOME CLOSING WORDS FROM PETER

After having had the opportunity to drink coffee with Peter and to hear from him concerning the divine nature, there is no doubt that you would be on fire for God and His Kingdom. Not only would you be fired up, but you would be headed in the right direction instead of trying to please God in the flesh. Most Christians continually frustrate the grace of God due to their zeal for God that is not according to knowledge. Remember…Peter told us that these things are acquired by and through the KNOWLEDGE of Him Who has called us to glory and virtue. Peter would probably leave you with some final statements concerning the divine nature. It is quite possible that he would say…"**For if these things be in you, and abound, they make you that you shall neither be barren nor unfruitful in the KNOWLEDGE of our Lord Jesus Christ. BUT he that lacks these things is blind, and cannot see afar off, and has forgotten that he was purged from his old sins. Wherefore the rather, brethren, give diligence to make your calling and election sure: for if you do these things, YOU SHALL NEVER FALL (2ND Peter 1:8-10)!!!**"

PART 14 - SONSHIP

<u>Sonship</u>: the state, fact, or relation of being a son. (Dictionary.com)

Romans 8:18-23 (Concordant Literal New Testament) states…"For I am reckoning that the sufferings of the current era do not deserve the glory about to be revealed for us. For the premonition of the creation is awaiting the unveiling of the sons of God. For to vanity was the creation subjected, not voluntarily, but because of Him Who subjects it, in expectation that the creation itself, also, shall be freed from the slavery of corruption into the glorious freedom of the children of God. For we are aware that the entire creation is groaning and travailing together until now. Yet not only so, but we ourselves also, who have the firstfruit of the spirit, we ourselves also, are groaning in ourselves, awaiting the **sonship**, the deliverance of our body."

The King James Version uses the word "adoption" instead of the word "sonship", which is used in the Concordant Literal New Testament. Either way, these English words come from the Greek word "huiothesia" (hwee-oth-es-ee'-ah), which means: "the placing of a fully grown mature son." It is so very important that we understand the teaching of sonship. It is only in and through the knowledge of sonship that we are able to grasp God dealing with us as sons. Many Christians who fail to recognize the process of sonship become discouraged in their walk with the Lord. They are unable to recognize that all the things they go through are God-ordained and are for a purpose. God's purpose in sonship is to grow us up in Him. During this process, we are brought from a child to a fully mature son of God. At the time of our ADOPTION, we will be <u>placed</u> (fully manifested) as the sons of God. The apostle Paul referred to this as THE MANIFESTATION OF THE SONS OF GOD. He also referred to this as the time when we would receive the REDEMPTION OF OUR BODIES. It is also important to note that we are already a son of God upon having placed our faith in the person and work of the Lord Jesus Christ (1st John 3:2). The only difference, though, is that we are not yet son-placed (fully matured and manifested). There is an appointed time for this to take place. We are not there yet. The important thing is for us to recognize that we are the sons of God and that we are being matured and conformed into the image of the Son of God. **Sonship is a process with a climax**. We must rightly divide God's Word, recognizing the difference between the two.

TEKNON VS. HUIOS

In order to discover the difference between what the Scriptures refer to as a child and a fully mature son of God, we must go to the original Greek. For example, 1st John 3:2 states…"Beloved, now are we the <u>sons</u> of God." The word "sons" in this verse comes from the Greek word "teknon". The word "teknon" means a child. This speaks of one who is a child of God, but is not yet fully matured or son-placed, whereas Romans 8:19 speaks of a fully mature son of God. Romans 8:19 states… "For the earnest expectation of the creature waits for the manifestation of the <u>sons</u> of God." The word "sons" in this verse comes from the Greek word "huios". The word "huios" means a fully grown son of God. Once again, this speaks of someone who has been son-placed.

According to Andrew Telford:

"In the early days of the Roman Empire when a boy was born into the family, he was cared for by his parents till he was twenty-one years of age. At the age of twenty-one, they took the child and placed him in the market place before the public. He was son-placed. From that time on he could sign his own name to legal documents, and went forward with the full authority of a man. This act at the market place did not make him a son; he was a son when he was born into his parents' family. At the age of twenty-one he was son-placed.

Adoption in the Bible means "son placed." I want you to notice Ephesians 2:7

7. "That in the ages to come He might show the exceeding riches of His grace in HIS kindness toward us through Christ Jesus."

That unfolding of the riches of His grace will be experienced by redeemed men when we are son-placed. May we again quote the definition? Adoption is a definite act of God whereby God sets a goal for the believer." -end quote- (<u>Subjects Of Sovereignty</u>, Andrew Telford)

We are now able to see the difference between a child and a fully grown son who has been son-placed. This is what it means to be in the process of sonship. Remember…**Sonship is a process with a climax**. We must recognize the process and the climax. During this process God deals with us in order to grow us up into the fullness of Who He is. In order for this to take place, the flesh must be dealt with. There is no other way. All of God's sons who are to be son-placed at the appointed time must die to their ways and be brought into the ways of the Spirit of God.

GOD DEALS WITH THE FLESH

Romans 7:18 gives us the grand and glorious revelation that was given to the apostle Paul concerning the futility of our fleshly efforts. It states…"For I know that in me (that is, in my flesh,) DWELLS NO GOOD THING: for to will is present with me; but how to perform that which is good I find not." Well…There you have it! Our problem is the flesh. The word "flesh" comes from the Greek word "sarx" and speaks of the carnal mind, including the corrupt nature of man. Paul even went on to say…"O wretched man that I am! Who shall deliver me from the body of this death (Romans 7:24)?" This is the first stop on the journey of sonship. We must come to the understanding that <u>our flesh is the enemy of God</u>! Most Christians remain as spiritual infants due to the fact that they never recognize their flesh as the enemy of God. They think that they are battling a Devil who is "out there somewhere", trying to "get them", not realizing that they have the properties of the Devil and the spirit of anti-Christ in their very flesh. Those who are being made into the image of the Son of God do not constantly blame everything on a Devil who is "out there somewhere", supposedly fighting against God, but rather, they have come to the revelation that the Devil (or Satan) is "the prince of the power of the air, THE <u>SPIRIT</u> THAT NOW WORKS IN THE CHILDREN OF DISOBEDIENCE (Ephesians 2:2)." In essence, the Devil is the spirit of opposition (created by God) that works in and through our flesh (carnal mind). What a revelation! Until this is realized, Christians will continue to remain as spiritual infants, saturated with self-righteousness, pointing their finger at everything and everyone but themselves, not realizing that their flesh is what is hindering them, not anyone or anything else. This is sonship and the way of the cross.

Those in the process of sonship are those who IDENTIFY with the death, burial, and resurrection of the Lord Jesus Christ. They do not merely look to or worship a historical Jesus Who is now supposed to be "somewhere way off up in the sky", but they have come to terms with the fact that the risen Christ is IN THEM, bringing them through the same process that the Son of God went through. They understand that Jesus was a PATTERN (SIGN) for all the sons of God to follow after. Jesus is not only their Savior, but He is their LORD AND KING, THEIR SOVEREIGN RULER. These sons of God are being brought to the place where they will relinquish their way, their will, and their kingdom.

They shall say…"May it not be my will, but may God's will be done." In essence, sonship is the Lordship of Jesus Christ that is to be manifested in and through a people. IT IS NOT AN EGO TRIP, BUT IT IS JUST THE OPPOSITE! It is humility, brokenness, and being crushed and consumed by our fiery trials brought on by the consuming fire of God. It involves temptation, testing, chastening, correction, and submission. Bill Britton referred to it as **THE HARNESS OF THE LORD**. It is the time of qualification for the sons of God that are to rule and reign with Jesus Christ now and in the ages to come. For the time being, the sons of God are as horses that have been harnessed for the purpose of training, but when the appointed time of their adoption comes they will be the very ones to pull the King's carriage. Remember…"If we suffer with Him, we shall also reign with Him (2nd Timothy 2:12)." All that has just been said can be summed up in three words. They are: **humility, submission, and partaking**. The end result is **exaltation, authority, and manifestation**.

JUSTIFICATION, SANCTIFICATION, AND GLORIFICATION

The sons of God are also able to see through the false message of the modern day church, which states that we are being saved from a torture pit in the middle of the earth. This false teaching of eternal torture has caused more spiritual ruin down through history than any other false teaching to date. God's company of sons has been awakened to the true Gospel of Jesus Christ, realizing that **JESUS DIED ON THE CROSS TO SAVE US FROM A CONDITION, NOT A LOCATION**. The false message of today's church states that Jesus died on the cross to save us from being eternally burned forever and ever in literal fire in an actual torture pit (referred to as hell) that is supposed to be located in the middle of the earth. **When this message is researched back to its origin, it will be found to be absolutely asinine, utterly ridiculous, based on Bible mistranslations, fueled by the carnal mind, and completely untrue!** So…What is the true message? The true message is sonship, of course, but let us get a little more specific as to what happens to the believer during this process.

In order to understand what happens during sonship we must first understand that we are a three-part being made up of spirit, soul, and body (1st Thessalonians 5:23). Now…If this is the case, and it is, then we must be saved spirit, soul, and body in order for the salvation process to be complete. Since Evangelical Christianity (for the most part) teaches that we are saved from eternal hell (which teaching is unscriptural), they miss the whole idea of what the Bible actually teaches about salvation.

Once again, the Bible teaches that we are saved from our condition of sin and death to the righteousness and life of the Son of God. The key is in understanding that this does not take place all at once. It actually happens in three phases. They are referred to as **justification, sanctification, and glorification**. These three experiences in God bring about the salvation of our spirit, soul, and body.

When a person believes on the Lord Jesus Christ he is justified (declared righteous based on his faith in the work / cross of the Lord Jesus Christ). The believer is a new creature in Christ, having had his spirit awakened, but he is not yet sanctified (made righteous). He has merely been declared righteous (on credit) based on his faith in the Son of God. But God does not stop there. He brings the believer to the next step. He actually wants us to **become** what we have been declared to be. Sanctification is really the heart of our salvation experience. During sanctification God deals with our soul (mind, will, and emotions), causing us to see that we must submit to having the spirit of the law written on our hearts in order to be conformed into the image of the Son of God (Jeremiah 31:31-33). It is during this time that we grow up in God, going from glory to glory, EVEN AS BY THE SPIRIT OF THE LORD (2nd Corinthians 3:18). The final step in sonship pertains to the redemption of our bodies. This is yet for an appointed time. Paul referred to it as the "manifestation of the sons of God" ("the adoption"). It is the time when all the overcomers shall come forth into the visible realm with glorified bodies in order to gather all nations into the government of God. At this time the sons of God shall be son-placed, being able to go forth without the limitations of the flesh. This is the beginning of the ministry of the ages to come (the ages of the ages), also referred to as the Feast of Tabernacles. The manifested sons of God shall rule and reign on the earth with the Lord Jesus Christ until every knee bows and every tongue confesses that Jesus Christ is Lord to the glory of God the Father. Those who will be son-placed during this time will be those who SUBMITTED to the process of sonship.

SOME CLOSING WORDS FROM BILL BRITTON

According to Bill Britton:

"There is a terrific operation of the Spirit going on today to bring the Sons of God into an absolute confinement to the perfect will of God. This is the Day of His Preparation, the day in which He is preparing the channel through which He shall pour forth His Glory for all the world to see. This channel is His Body in the earth, that glorious company of people who are being conformed through much tribulation and fiery tests to the image of the Son of God. This is His "battle axe and weapons of war" with which He shall subdue kingdoms and overcome all His enemies. This is His "mighty and strong One" to whom He shall commit the work of judging this world. This is His Overcomer, His "great army" with which He shall bring the nations into submission. The weapons of their warfare are not carnal, natural weapons but they are mighty weapons, mighty through God to the pulling down of strongholds. These are those who shall "be strong and do exploits."

But before God can commit this great and tremendous ministry into their hands they must submit themselves to the discipline of the Lord, letting Him truly be the Lord of their entire lives. We have long since dealt with the question of open sin, but now God is dealing with the inward rebellion of our own wills. Some good Christians are not now being so dealt with, for they are not in this Firstfruits Company, but nevertheless there is a real dealing of God going on within those who are called into the High Calling of God. This is a very real thing and is the work of the Refiner's Fire. To those who are going through it, some of its aspects are horrible, but very necessary, and the end result thereof is glorious as we are brought into absolute and complete submission to the will of our Lord." -end quote- (The Harness Of The Lord, Bill Britton)

PART 15 - THE LOVE OF GOD

No written work on Biblical subjects would be complete without drawing the reader's attention to the most important topic in the Bible. In order to understand God we must seek to understand His love. It is not that God has love, or that He is loving, but **GOD IS LOVE!** With this in mind, we should ever seek to grasp, bask in, receive, and distribute this love that GOD IS. Too much of that which is taught in Christianity presents a God Who has love, or loves to a certain degree, but this God (the God of the modern church) is not presented as Someone Who IS LOVE, AND WHO IS A LOVE THAT **NEVER FAILS**. If we are to ever make an impact on the world, then we must come to terms with the fact that we, in and of ourselves, are bankrupt and void of this love that God is. This causes us to open ourselves up to God's divine nature and character, which is love. We then become partakers of His divine nature and character. This causes us to actually become like Him and to become what He is. It is only by believing, receiving, and distributing the love of God that the world will know that we are the true disciples of Jesus Christ (John 13:35). Everything else is nothing more than a religious facade and will only bring about spiritual ruin and death. According to the apostle Paul, without the love of God in our hearts WE ARE NOTHING! Without God's love we are nothing more than a noisy gong or a clanging cymbal (1st Corinthians 13:1-2). Let us realize the importance of grasping the nature and character of our Heavenly Father, for without a knowledge of the love that He is, we really do not know Him, and our Christian walk in this life is in vain.

ROOTED AND GROUNDED IN LOVE

Ephesians 3:17-19 states…"That Christ may dwell in your hearts by faith; that you, being rooted and grounded in love, may be able to comprehend with all saints what is the breadth, and length, and depth, and height; and to know the love of Christ, which passes knowledge, that you might be filled with all the fullness of God." In order to make this passage a little more clear, here is verse 19 as it reads from the Amplified Bible…"[That you may really come] to know [practically, through experience for yourselves] **the love of Christ, which far surpasses mere knowledge [without experience]**; that you may be filled [through all your being] unto all the fullness of God [may have the richest measure of the divine Presence, and become a body wholly filled and flooded with God Himself]!" As we can see from the following passage, God's love is something that must be EXPERIENCED. The experience of God's love goes far beyond mere knowledge. In essence, His love must be revealed to us. After having it revealed to us, we then have an experiential knowledge of the reality of His love. We are then able to believe the love that God has for us and others, extending it to others. The apostle John put it this way…"And we have known and believed the love that God has to us. **God is love**; and he that dwells in love dwells in God, and God in him (1st John 4:16)." As well, John would go on to say…"WE LOVE HIM, **BECAUSE HE FIRST LOVED US** (1st John 4:19)." These are the first steps that must be taken in order to embrace the love of God. We must realize that God is love, we do not have His love, and that His love must be revealed to us, causing us to know (by experience) and believe the love that He has for us because of His very nature and character. In essence, He loves us because He is God, and God is love.

EXPLAINING THE LOVE OF GOD

There are many statements that we could make concerning the love of God, such as…Love is the nature and character of God…Love is a Person (the Lord Jesus Christ)…and, of course…God is love. These are all good ways to explain the love of God, but let us try to go into a little more detail as to how God's love (nature and character) is extended and distributed to, in, and through us. We would have to say that God's very essence is that of love. Remember…It is not that He has love toward us, but that HE IS LOVE! There are many other attributes that flow from God's love, but do not necessarily define Who He is. For example, God may exercise His wrath, judgment, vengeance, or punishment toward men, but God cannot be defined by these attributes. God is not wrath or vengeance. GOD IS LOVE! These attributes (and all the other attributes of God) must be defined as coming forth from the very love of God. God's wrath, judgment, vengeance, and punishment are all attributes of His love that are exercised toward sinful men for the purpose of correction and restoration. This is how we must expound on the love of God. Many Christians claim that God is love, but that He is also a God of judgment. While it is true that God does administer judgment, it is not proper to say that God is judgment. The proper thing to say is that God is love, and that judgment flows from His love for the purpose of correction. When we begin to see Him in this light, we will understand that God is good and right in all His ways, and that all His ways are motivated by His nature and character, which is LOVE. Every attribute of God (including wrath, judgment, vengeance, and punishment) flows out of His nature and character, which is love.

So…When we say…"the love of God", we are actually speaking of the nature and character of God. Now…Let's go a little deeper in our explanation. **The key that unlocks the understanding of God, Who is love, is in knowing that our Heavenly Father (according to His nature, which is love) is <u>corrective</u> in all His ways, not vindictive!!!** This means that it is IMPOSSIBLE for the teaching of eternal torture to be correct. Every teaching or doctrine must come in line with the nature and character of God, Who is love. The church has taught for centuries that God's judgments are vindictive in nature rather than corrective. This can be traced back to Augustine, the Catholic Church, the Dark Ages, mistranslations in the King James Version, and the carnal mind. This is the exact opposite of what the Bible actually teaches, but the traditions and doctrines of men are very powerful to the carnal mind. This means that all of God's dealings with man are to be found within the ages of time and for the purpose of correction. There is no vindictiveness that is to be found in His nature. God is not out for revenge, nor does He have a vindictive spirit. Many in Christianity have bought into the LIE that God is like man, in that He is out for revenge and eager to eternally torture all those who do not obey Him. What could ever be accomplished by torturing someone forever? Is that love? Is that the nature and character of our Heavenly Father? When will we **wake up** and see that our Heavenly Father is not like us. He is not out for revenge. He is not vindictive like we are. He is corrective! He is love! He is merciful! He is God!

AGAPE

As we have already stated, 1ˢᵗ John 4:16 tells us that "God is love." The word "love" in this verse comes from the Greek word "agape". "Agape" is one of several Greek words translated into English as love. The word has been used in different ways by a variety of contemporary and ancient sources, including Biblical authors. Many have thought that **this word represents divine, unconditional, self-sacrificing, active, volitional, and thoughtful love** (definition of "agape" taken from Wikipedia Encyclopedia). The word "agape" speaks of a love that is all giving, not getting. This love, which flows from God's very nature, is God's disposition toward the human race. His nature toward us is one of always doing what is best for us, not based on feeling or merit. He simply loves us because HE IS LOVE, not because we have earned or can earn His love. When we do right God loves us. When we do wrong God loves us. When we believe on Him God loves us. When we reject

Him and deny His existence God loves us. His love for us never changes because it is the very essence of His nature to love us. The only thing that we can do is to love Him back because He first loved us. His love waits to be discovered, embraced, distributed, and returned back to Him. The words of the apostle John from 1st John 4:19 are so beautiful that I must quote them again…"**WE LOVE HIM, BECAUSE HE FIRST LOVED US!**" This is the very heart of the Gospel. This is what it is all about. It is all about God, and God is love. He is loving the creation unto Himself. His love was manifested in and through the cross of the Lord Jesus Christ. 1st John 4:9 states…"In this was manifested the love of God toward us, BECAUSE that God sent His only begotten Son into the world, that we might live through Him." There is also much that we can learn about God's "agape" love from 1st Corinthians chapter thirteen.

LOVE (GOD) NEVER FAILS

1st Corinthians chapter thirteen gives us a detailed explanation of the love of God. It starts out by telling us that we can possess any and all spiritual gifts, but if we do not have God's love (nature and character) in our hearts, then all of our living is in vain. It even goes on to say that we can do the right thing, being motivated by the wrong reason. This statement gets to the very heart of the matter. The chief aim of our Heavenly Father is to put His love in our heart. To operate in the love of God is to know Him, to be like Him, and is the defining aspect of a true disciple of Jesus Christ. All else is dung (according to the apostle Paul in Philippians 3:8)!

Verses four through eight of this chapter go into great detail concerning the outworking of God's love. These verses tell us that…"Love endures long and is patient and kind; love never is envious nor boils over with jealousy, is not boastful or vainglorious, does not display itself haughtily. It is not conceited (arrogant and inflated with pride); it is not rude (unmannerly) and does not act unbecomingly. Love (God's love in us) does not insist on its own rights or its own way, for it is not self-seeking; it is not touchy or fretful or resentful; it takes no account of the evil done to it [it pays no attention to a suffered wrong]. It does not rejoice at injustice and unrighteousness, but rejoices when right and truth prevail. Love bears up under anything and everything that comes, is ever ready to believe the best of every person, its hopes are fadeless under all circumstances, and it endures everything [without weakening]. **Love never fails [never fades out or becomes obsolete or comes to an end]** (The Amplified Bible)."

After such a passage as this, my next question would be…How could we ever doubt God's good intentions for us, or doubt that God's love would ever fail or give up on any one person of the human race? His love is undeniable, unstoppable, unbelievable, incredible, beyond words, without limit, and **INESCAPABLE!!!** I can personally assure you the reader that our Heavenly Father's love WILL NEVER FAIL! HIS LOVE REACHES TO THE HIGHEST MOUNTAIN AND TO THE LOWEST HELL! THERE IS NO ONE WHO (AT THE END OF TIME) WILL BE ABLE TO DEFEAT HIS INESCAPABLE LOVE! GOD'S LOVE WILL PROVE TO BE TOO PASSIONATE AND FIERCE TO RESIST WHEN IT IS REVEALED TO EVERY MAN IN THE AGES TO COME! OH HOW I WISH I HAD THE VOCABULARY TO EXPOUND UPON HIS AMAZING LOVE! **WE CAN REST ASSURED THAT GOD'S LOVE WILL EVENTUALLY DRAW ALL MEN UNTO HIM, FOR IF EVEN ONE SOUL REMAINS OUTSIDE OF THE LOVE OF GOD AT THE END OF TIME, THEN THAT ONE PERSON HAS DEFEATED GOD. THAT, MY FRIEND, IS IMPOSSIBLE, FOR GOD IS A LOVE THAT NEVER FAILS. IF HIS LOVE FAILS TO REACH EVEN ONE PERSON, THEN HE WOULD CEASE TO BE GOD, FOR GOD IS LOVE!**

The following people are quoted in this book. The teachings in which they are quoted are listed after their name. If the quote came from a specific book, article, or work it is listed after the quote.

Adams, A. P.: Part 1

Amirault, Gary: Part 5

Britton, Bill: Part 4, Part 14

Christian Apologetics & Research Ministries: Part 11

Dever, William G.: Part 5

Garganta, Richard Wayne: Part 5

Gavazzoni, John: Part 5

Hall, Elvina M.: Part 10

Jacobovici, Simcha: Part 5

Jones, Dr. Stephen: Part 5, Part 9

Kloner, Amos: Part 5

Magness, Jodi: Part 5

Newman, Keith: Part 11

Paul, The Apostle: Part 5

Telford, Andrew: Part 14

The Christian Arsenal: Part 5

Thomas M. D., John: Part 9

Zender, Martin: Part 3

Zias, Joe: Part 5

ORDER FORM

THE NOBLE BEREAN SERIES VOLUME 1

Send this form, a photocopy of this form or a letter containing the information requested below to:

Straightway Publishing Company
P.O. Box 45212 #261
Baton Rouge, LA. 70895

Enclose a check or money order for $12.95, payable to Straightway Publishing Company. Straightway Publishing Company will pay shipping and handling and any sales taxes.

Fill in name and address where the book is to be shipped:

Name:_____

Address:_____

City:_____ State:_____ Zip:_____

In case of questions concerning your order, please give your phone number and Email address:

Telephone:_____

Email address:_____

If you have any questions, Straightway Publishing Company can be reached by calling (225) 766-0896.

If this book is unsatisfactory for any reason
you may return it for a full refund.

http://www.hearingthetruthofgod.com/

www.ingramcontent.com/pod-product-compliance
Ingram Content Group UK Ltd.
Pitfield, Milton Keynes, MK11 3LW, UK
UKHW021309180426
11947UKWH00015B/1107